COOK THAI

I would like to dedicate this book to my grandmother. My first memories of enjoying cooking, baking and eating are with her and my mum, so this one's for her. However, if she was around today she would probably be wondering why the bloody hell I'm cooking Thai food for a living and not baking. I'm pretty sure I used to ask her to make me chocolate cake for dinner when I was a kid.

First published in Great Britain in 2017 by
Kyle Books, an imprint of Kyle Cathie Ltd
192–198 Vauxhall Bridge Road
London SW1V 1DX
general.enquiries@kylebooks.com
www.kylebooks.co.uk

10 9 8 7 6 5 4 3 2 1

ISBN 978 0 85783 394 5

Editor: Judith Hannam
Editorial Assistant: Hannah Coughlin
Copy Editor: Corinne Masciocchi
Designer: Evi O
Photographer: Tom Regester
Food Stylist: Becks Wilkinson
Prop Stylist: Luis Peral
Production: Nic Jones and Gemma John

A Cataloguing in Publication record for this title is available from the British Library.

Colour reproduction by ALTA London
Printed and bound in China by 1010 Printing International Limited

COOK THAI

SET YOUR TASTE BUDS ON FIRE WITH
100 DELICIOUS, MODERN DISHES

SEBBY HOLMES

Photography by Tom Regester

KYLE BOOKS

INTRODUCTION

I find it very amusing seeing the look on people's faces when they ask how many years I've spent In Thailand learning to cook, and I respond with, 'I actually learned how to cook Thai food in Peckham'.

I still consider myself an accidental chef. In my time, I have wanted to be many things: a palaeontologist (don't ask!), a travel writer and a food critic, but despite this I have spent more than half my life cooking in professional kitchens. I fell in love with food when I stepped into my first pub kitchen in Oxfordshire to do work experience when I was a kid. Since then, I have been cooking either full or part time, breaking only to travel and get a degree in Journalism from Kingston University. Not that this helped with my spelling or grammar – I'm sure the copy editor for this book had a nightmare! There is no doubt about it, I fell naturally into the world of hospitality and my bond with it grows stronger every day. I love it.

When I finished university, I knew I wanted to cook and I also knew I wanted to write. I had no idea, however, about all the bits in between, so I packed my bag full of chef whites and knives and, armed with my CV, stomped my way towards the bright lights of London. Almost immediately, I found myself at the Begging Bowl in Peckham. I considered myself experienced as a chef, but this kitchen put me back in my place. I felt like a baby again, every ingredient was a new taste and smell for me to explore. It was here that my knowledge and understanding of good quality Thai food developed into a passion, one that I have now devoted my career to. I was lucky enough to work closely with some amazing people who taught me a lot about the cuisine, the culture and Thai cooking methods. Some of them have been nice enough to contribute a recipe to this book.

After a few years honing in my skills, I was delighted to get asked to join the Smoking Goat Soho as the head chef for the launch of their Thai street food barbecue restaurant. This was a smash hit and still is. There we fused slow-cooked barbecue meats with funky Thai flavours in some incredible ways. In early 2016, I started my own Thai street food restaurant concept called Farang London, this has accelerated quickly and we are soon to open our third kitchen across London. We focus on making everything we possibly can ourselves and using only the best quality ingredients we can get our hands on. We hold no loyalty to authenticity, just to taste and flavour.

Throughout the last few years I have tasted and developed many recipes that even when I get home I cannot be without. I think the diversity of Thai food makes it something that should be eaten a few times a week, not just for a special occasion. The recipes in this book are a collection of my most loved meals to cook at home and it's been an absolute pleasure putting them in a cookbook. I hope you enjoy cooking them as much as I do.

KITCHEN
BITS

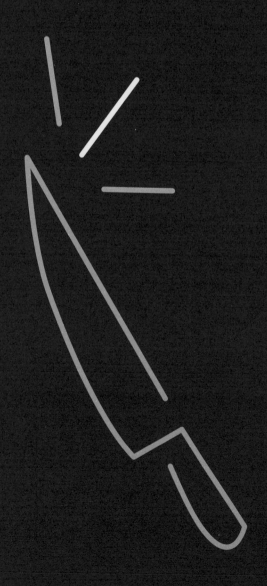

There is so much fun to be had when cooking Thai food at home. From deep-frying whole pork bellies to smashing out fresh papaya salads, it's an exciting way to get stuck into the kitchen and create some tasty results. I've learned through experience that there are a few things worth knowing when thinking about cooking Thai food on a regular basis.

One of the most eye opening was how easy it was to make my own coconut cream. Initially, it appeared to be a very daunting task – I'm not sure about you, but having to attack a fruit with a hammer to cook was a first! However, I learned that making coconut cream is a very simple process and if you are only making it for a few people it can be quick. The difference in taste between fresh coconut cream and tinned is remarkable; they are worlds apart. Don't get me wrong, it's not always feasible to make your own cream from scratch, but it is certainly worth a go on a rainy day.

COCONUT CREAM

To make 500ml of coconut cream you will need 5 coconuts, a hammer, a butter knife, a peeler, a grater, a stick blender, a straining cloth and 2 litres of water.

Start by cracking the coconuts with a hammer; be sure to wear thick rubber gloves to protect your hands. Holding the coconut in one hand, carefully hammer the coconut until it cracks around the outside. Continue to hammer it until the crack is large enough to insert a butter knife and the crack goes around all or most of the coconut. Next, using the tip of the butter knife, separate the tough outer shell of the coconut from the soft flesh within. The inner flesh has an inedible skin attached to it. Use a peeler to remove this skin, leaving just the white coconut flesh. Discard the outer shell.

Next put this flesh through a mincer, or grate it and add it to 2 litres of boiling water. Combine thoroughly using a stick blender for around 5 minutes. Once combined, filter the liquid from the flesh by ringing it out in a cloth or through a sieve. Once separated, place the liquid in the fridge and leave to cool. As it cools the cream will separate from the water; the white cream will sit at the top and the coconut milk will sit at the bottom. Separate the cream from the milk using a ladle.

Now this is where it really gets interesting, as there is a range of products that can be made from both the cream and the milk. The cream is mainly used for thickening and sweetening curries, soups and sauces, the milk to let out curries and soups. Any leftover coconut cream can be boiled down until it splits. In my experience this has always been known as coconut crack, which is essentially coconut oil. This is commonly used to cook out curry pastes and stir fries, it also freezes very well. Lastly, the leftover grated coconut can be toasted and used within salads, or thrown over an open fire to create flavoured smoke.

DRIED SPICES

Another thing I find more and more important every day is drying your own ingredients and spices whenever possible. Not only does this cut down on waste, as you can use up old produce, the flavours are much more intense than those of pre-prepared spices sold in supermarkets. You can really taste the difference when you use your own dried spices. Lots of the recipes in this book use certain dried spices regularly, so why not have the good stuff to hand.

For me, the three essentials are red turmeric, ginger and galangal, and all three require the same preparation, which is minimal. Firstly, you need to peel them, then slice them as thin as you can with a knife. If your knife skills are not great then it's probably best to use either a peeler or a mandoline so you can be sure that all the slices are uniformly thin. Now lay these slices out on a raised rack, to allow air to circulate around them. Leave them in a warm dry place for around 48 hours – I use the airing cupboard at home. After this time the pieces should be shrivelled and dry and very slightly discoloured. If they aren't, leave for a further 12 hours.

Once dried, grind them one at a time in a pestle and mortar or a spice grinder to a fine powder, then store in an airtight container. They will keep indefinitely, though the flavour will slowly fade over time.

BRINING

People have written entire books on the topic of brining, so if you are really interested in it I would recommend doing some wider reading on the subject. It's a fascinating cooking technique that, in a nutshell, adds flavour to meat and allows it to be cooked at higher temperatures for longer without drying out. It's therefore an ideal technique to use when slow roasting large joints of meat or cooking over an open flame or a barbecue. When you really get to grips with the brining process the salt content in the brining solution can be changed, as can the length of time the meat is brined for. Different flavours can also be added to the brining solution to alter the final taste of the meat.

My failsafe brining solution is a great thing to have lying around in the fridge, particularly since, as it's basically salt and sugar, it'll keep indefinitely. If I have them lying around at the time, I'll also add pandanus leaves, galangal stems, lemongrass sheaths, garlic cloves, kaffir lime leaves. These are not essential, but a brine is certainly a good way to use up some of the waste left over after cooking with these ingredients or making a curry paste.

To make around 1 litre of brine, bring 1 litre of water to the boil in a large pot, add 100g caster sugar, 100g table salt and a selection of any of the ingredients listed above that you have to hand. Bring back to a simmer on a medium heat, stirring regularly until the salt and sugar have completely dissolved. Allow to cool, then either use straight away or refrigerate.

This is a basic, 10 per cent salt solution brine, which is quite strong. To put it into perspective, seawater is around 3 per cent salt and we've all accidently swallowed that before! I would allow 1 hour's brining time for every kilogram of meat in a brine this strong. Also, when brining any meat, make sure that every piece is submerged in the brine so that the solution can fully take effect.

DEEP FRYING

Say these words to a British cook and most will think 'fish and chips', however in Thailand deep frying ingredients in oil is a cooking technique that has many different methods and applications. In most cases, the best equipment to use is a large wok full of oil and a spider (perforated spoon), with which to remove the deep-fried ingredients. This allows for a larger open surface area when frying, giving the cook a better chance of controlling the oil temperature.

Over the last few years I have continued to be amazed by the techniques used for frying ingredients in Thai cuisine. From whole fish to whole joints of meat, tempura vegetables to crispy basil leaves and deep-fried chilli jam to whole peanuts, it's well worth investing in some proper equipment to ensure you can master this technique at home with ease.

THE PESTLE & MORTAR

Now I'm not going to bore you with all the usual mumbo jumbo around all the different types of pestles and mortars that seems to be in every introduction to most Thai cookbooks. However, I do feel it's necessary to stress the importance of buying a large, granite pestle and mortar; it will make cooking the recipes in this book much easier. Also, in my opinion, there is no more effective or exciting way to combine ingredients than through using brute force. Many chefs will say you can use a food processor instead, which in some cases you can, though you'll never achieve the same consistency as you will using a pestle and mortar as you can only chop ingredients.

These are just a few helpful pointers that are worth knowing before getting started cooking Thai food at home. This is a cuisine that I have fallen in love with and when you start getting stuck in you will too. Its varied cooking styles and flavours take you on a journey without even needing to leave your own kitchen, so what are you waiting for – get cooking!

1 SNACK & NIBBLES

CRISPY PORK BELLY
WITH SPICY RELISH

200g table salt

200g caster sugar

4 kaffir lime leaves,
torn a little

3 sticks lemongrass, bruised

500g ice cubes

400g pork belly, skin scored

1 teaspoon coarse sea salt

10g chopped coriander,
to garnish

2 spring onions, finely sliced,
to garnish

SPICY RELISH

3 banana shallots, unpeeled

1 head of garlic, unpeeled
and broken into cloves

60g cherry tomatoes

3 green bird's-eye chillies

6 yellow wax pepper chillies
or banana pepper

30g palm sugar (or soft light
brown sugar)

20ml tamarind water

1 teaspoon distilled
white vinegar

10ml fish sauce

It takes a little bit of time to get this pork belly dish on the plate but it is very easy to make. Brining it fills the meat with moisture and flavour and produces amazing results when roasted. If you have the time, it's worth grilling the vegetables for the relish over a wood barbecue as it adds an unmissable smokiness.

In a large, deep saucepan, heat 1½ litres water with the table salt, sugar, kaffir lime leaves and 1 of the lemongrass sticks, stirring regularly so that the solids don't collect on the bottom of the pan and the heat is distributed evenly. When everything has melted, remove from the heat and add the ice cubes. When cool, submerge the pork belly in the salt solution and refrigerate for 2 hours to brine.

After 2 hours, remove the pork from the solution and discard the liquid. Pat the pork dry with a tea towel or dry cloth and refrigerate for a further hour to ensure it is completely dry.

Preheat the oven to 180°C/gas mark 4. Rub the coarse sea salt into the pork belly skin to help it crisp up during cooking and place in a roasting tray. Transfer to the top shelf of the oven and roast for 2–2½ hours, depending on the fat content of the meat. Make sure you check the pork every 30 minutes after the first hour. It is ready when the juices run clear, the meat is piping hot throughout and the skin is golden brown and crispy. Remove from the oven, wrap in clingfilm and leave to rest for 20 minutes.

Meanwhile, make the relish. This can be made on a barbecue, but it is also great made in the oven. Place the banana shallots, the remaining lemongrass, the garlic, cherry tomatoes, chillies and wax pepper chillies in a roasting tray, then wrap the tray in foil and transfer to the oven (while the pork is cooking). The vegetables will cook at different rates, so check them every 10 minutes, removing the ones that are soft first. The banana shallots and lemongrass will take the longest (35–40 minutes). Once all the ingredients have softened, peel the shallots and garlic, remove the stems from the chillies and peel the outer shell of the lemongrass. Chop the lemongrass a little to make it easier to work with.

In a pestle and mortar or food processor, pound together all the roasted ingredients to a chunky relish. Stir in the palm sugar while the relish is still warm, then add the tamarind water, vinegar and fish sauce and combine well. Taste the relish and make sure it is seasoned as you like it; I like it sweet, salty, spicy and sour, with an edge towards the salty and sour.

Unwrap the pork belly from the clingfilm and slice it thinly. Serve alongside the relish and sprinkle with the coriander and spring onions.

TIGER PRAWN AND
SWEET POTATO FRITTERS
WITH SWEET CHILLI JAM

SERVES 2   GF
WITH PLENTY OF CURRY POWDER
LEFT FOR THE CUPBOARD

3 teaspoons coriander seeds

I teaspoon cloves

I teaspoon fennel seeds

3 teaspoons cumin seeds

8 cardamom pods,
husks removed

I teaspoon black
peppercorns

5 teaspoons ground ginger

7 teaspoons ground turmeric

4 teaspoons chilli powder,
(see intro)

2 quantities sweet chilli jam
(see page 150)

I lime, cut into wedges,
to serve

FOR THE FRITTERS

5 tablespoons rice flour

a pinch of sea salt

100ml sparkling water

2 medium free-range eggs

6 tiger prawns, shelled and
deveined, but tails and heads
attached

I large sweet potato,
peeled and julienned

20g Thai sweet basil,
plus extra to garnish

2 litres sunflower oil

Homemade chilli power is always preferable. In the industry, we make it using dried chillies and call it 'blue tongue'. I have no idea why or where the term came from. I assume it's something to do with the fact that it's fucking hot and will leave you with a burning mouth if you're not careful. The best way to make it at home is to dry fry dried chillies on a high heat before grinding to a powder using a pestle and mortar. Keep them moving until they start to smoke and colour, and then cover with foil and place in an oven preheated to 180°C to toast a little further. Take care. If you breathe in the smoke, you will cough. I also like to use 50/50 dried bird's eye chillies to dried long red chillies as this gives the chilli powder a fiery hot, smoky and sweet flavour.

First get the curry powder made. Have all the spices measured out before you start then place a large frying pan on a low heat. When toasting spices, you should always heat them in order of their size: larger spices first and for longer. So begin with the coriander seeds and follow with the cloves, fennel, cumin and cardamom. When a spice begins to change colour and release a fragrant smell, it is ready to use. The only spices that should not be toasted according to size are black peppercorns as they pop and explode; just add them at the end, turn off the heat, and let the other spices warm them through. Next, add the ginger, turmeric and chilli powder then grind everything together to make the curry powder.

Next make the fritters. In a mixing bowl, whisk together I tablespoon of the homemade curry powder, the rice flour, sea salt, sparkling water and eggs. Beat to a pale mixture, then rest in the fridge for a few minutes. In a separate mixing bowl, combine the prawns, sweet potato and basil. Pour the batter over this, then mix with your hands until everything is coated in the egg mixture.

Heat the oil in a deep saucepan to 180°C. Use a sieve or kitchen spider to gently lower spoonfuls of the mixture into the oil, making sure that the fritters remain in one piece. Cook one at a time for 2–3 minutes, moving regularly to ensure even cooking, then drain on kitchen paper.

Serve the fritters garnished with the basil and eat it with sweet chilli. It's also awesome with a big squeeze of lime juice.

POMEGRANATE MIANG BITES

30g whole peanuts

50g desiccated coconut

200g palm sugar (or soft light brown sugar)

50ml fish sauce (soy sauce if vegetarian)

50g tamarind paste

20g pomegranate seeds

½ lime, diced with skin still on

2 red bird's-eye chillies, thinly sliced

20g ginger, peeled and diced

10g coriander leaves, chopped

20g Thai shallots, peeled and sliced (or 1 banana shallot)

2 heads of baby gem lettuce, separated into leaves (or betel leaves)

Miang is one of my favourite dishes. It's an absolute flavour bomb – sweet, salty, sour and spicy, yet fresh and light at the same time. I always have a laugh with the bird's eye chillies when friends are around, as it can be extremely entertaining to (accidently) put a little extra in their portion. My friends at *Thai Smile* magazine tell me that in Thailand this dish is commonly made with the help of the kids at home as it is fun and interactive. Traditionally, it uses pomelo and betel leaves, or a range of sweet and sour fruits, but I find it delicious with pomegranate.

Preheat the oven to 180°C/gas mark 4. Place the peanuts on a baking tray on the top shelf of the oven and the coconut on the bottom shelf and toast for about 15 minutes, shaking the trays every 5 minutes to ensure that the nuts and coconut toast evenly. They are ready when both are golden brown.

Place the palm sugar and fish sauce (or soy sauce) in a medium non-stick saucepan and warm over a moderate heat, stirring regularly until the sugar has melted and the mixture begins to bubble gently. Remove from the heat.

In a food processor, blitz the coconut and peanuts together, then add these to the palm sugar and fish sauce mixture and return to a low heat. Bring back to a gentle boil, then remove from the heat, add the tamarind paste, stir and allow to cool. The mixture should be rich and sticky, and as it cools it should thicken and the peanuts and coconut should settle on the top. At this stage the miang sauce can be kept in the fridge for use later (if placed in a sterilised jar it will keep indefinitely).

When ready to serve, mix all the remaining ingredients together in a large bowl. Give the miang sauce a stir, then add it to the other ingredients, using a spoon to gently mix it through the fresh ingredients.

Serve the baby gem leaves piled up nicely on a plate, alongside the miang mixture and allow guests to get stuck in. Alternatively, you can place a portion of the mixture on each leaf and serve as a posh canapé.

SPICED AUBERGINES
WITH YELLOW BEANS

500ml sunflower oil

2 Thai purple aubergines, sliced into 5 x 2cm matchsticks

6 garlic cloves, peeled

3 long green chillies, stems and seeds removed and roughly chopped

2 tablespoons chopped coriander roots

½ teaspoon coarse sea salt

1 tablespoon vegetable oil

20g yellow bean paste

1 tablespoon caster sugar

juice of ½ lime

¼ teaspoon white peppercorns, toasted and ground to a fine powder

1 teaspoon distilled white vinegar

20ml vegetable stock

10g coriander, roughly chopped

1 teaspoon soy sauce

Aubergines are interesting to cook with as they react so differently, depending on the method you use. When grilled or barbecued they almost melt inside their skins and take on a smoky flavour and soft texture. When fried and then stir-fried, as in this recipe, they keep their shape and act like little sponges, soaking up all the flavour from the yellow bean sauce. These are great as a side or a snack.

Have a tray lined with kitchen paper at the ready and heat the sunflower oil in a large saucepan to about 220°C. Test a piece of aubergine first to check that the oil is at the correct temperature: if it shrivels and turns black, allow the oil to cool slightly before using. Cook the aubergines for 1–1½ minutes, until they are golden brown on the outside, then remove from the heat and drain on the prepared tray.

Pound the garlic, chillies and coriander roots to a paste in a large pestle and mortar or food processor, using the salt as an abrasive, if necessary. In a large wok, heat the vegetable oil and fry the paste in the oil until it begins to turn golden brown, then add the yellow bean paste and fry for a further 6–8 minutes until the paste darkens slightly and begins to smell like miso. Add the sugar, lime juice, white peppercorns, vinegar, stock, coriander, soy sauce and the hot aubergines, then toss to combine all the ingredients. Taste for seasoning: it should be salty, sweet and mild with a hint of sourness. Serve immediately.

TIPS

When cooking with tough and fibrous ingredients it is sometimes necessary to bruise them to release their flavours. Their thick outer casing acts as a barrier to the flavoursome core within. I always bruise galangal and lemongrass when adding to braising stocks and soups. The Thai people created the pestle and mortar for exactly this purpose.

FISH SAUCE SALTED BEEF WITH ROASTED CHILLI RELISH

1 tablespoon roughly chopped coriander roots

1 stick lemongrass, bruised

2 kaffir lime leaves, torn

4 garlic cloves, lightly bruised

2 long red chillies, charred in a dry pan and bruised

300ml fish sauce

2 tablespoons caster sugar

½ tablespoon whole cumin, toasted

4 beef cheeks (about 600–800g), skin removed

600g rendered beef fat (ask your butcher for this; or use vegetable oil)

10g coriander leaves, chopped, to garnish

FOR THE CHILLI RELISH

10 Thai shallots (or 3 banana shallots), unpeeled

4 garlic cloves, unpeeled

6 mixed green and red bird's-eye chillies

20ml thick tamarind water

10ml fish sauce

1 tablespoon roughly chopped coriander roots

6 dried long red chillies, gently toasted

30g palm sugar (or soft dark brown sugar)

a pinch of coarse sea salt

It takes a little time to confit the beef in this recipe but every second is worth the wait as marinating the meat in fish sauce makes it something special. It's also a great way to use some of the cheaper, slow cook cuts as the confit process breaks down the muscle tissue within the meat to the point where it melts in the mouth. A plate of this in any situation that does not involve vegetarians will not last long.

In a large bowl, mix the coriander roots, lemongrass, kaffir lime leaves, garlic, chillies, fish sauce, caster sugar and cumin. Add the beef and submerge it in the marinade, ensuring it is thoroughly coated. Cover with clingfilm and refrigerate for a minimum of 3 hours, but ideally overnight. After this time, remove the beef and use a sieve to discard the liquid of the marinade, keeping the aromatics for the confit process.

Preheat the oven to 100°C/gas mark ¼. To make the confit, melt the beef fat in a heavy-based ovenproof casserole and add all the aromatics from the marinade (if using oil instead of beef fat, pour 600ml vegetable oil into the casserole). Add the beef, making sure that it is submerged in the hot fat/oil, then cover and transfer to the oven for 4–6 hours.

Meanwhile, make the chilli relish. In a dry frying pan over a high heat, add the shallots, shaking the pan regularly, then add the garlic and bird's-eye chillies. Keep all the ingredients moving in the pan; the idea is to char them all so that they colour on the outside and are soft on the inside. Remove the pan from the heat and allow to cool slightly, then peel the garlic and shallots and remove the chilli stems. Combine these ingredients in a pestle and mortar or food processor with the tamarind water, fish sauce, coriander roots, dried long red chillies and palm sugar, then continue to pound until you have a coarse relish, using a little coarse sea salt as an abrasive, if necessary (be careful though as the beef is already salted). The relish should be sweet, sour and fiery hot, with a little salt to round it off, but not too much as the beef is salted.

The beef is ready when the meat is so tender that you can cut it with a spoon. Remove from the oven and allow to cool slightly, then serve lightly pulled apart on a plate, sprinkled with coriander and with the relish on the side for dipping. If not eating immediately, allow the beef to cool, then refrigerate. The beef will keep for 6–8 days in the fridge.

MAKES ABOUT
500G
(ABOUT 25 SERVINGS)

2 litres sunflower oil

1 head of garlic, cloves
peeled and minced in a
food processor or pestle
and mortar

450g unsalted peanuts

10g dried shrimp,
ground to a floss

10 dried long red chillies,
toasted in a dry pan until
charred, then pounded to
a powder (use a little less
if you don't like it hot)

15 kaffir lime leaves, stems
removed and fine julienned

15g soft brown sugar

3 tablespoons fish sauce

a pinch of coarse sea salt

SHRIMP, KAFFIR LIME LEAVES, CHILLI AND GARLIC PEANUTS

These are the perfect accompaniment to a boozy evening with friends. The sweet, salty, savoury and aromatic flavours keep you coming back for more and keeps the beer flowing. They are also so simple to make you could probably even manage it after you have had a few.

Heat the oil in a large saucepan to about 180°C. Test the temperature by dropping in a teaspoon of minced garlic and seeing how it reacts: if it bubbles gently, then the temperature is perfect for cooking, so add all the minced garlic and carefully stir it with a fork, making sure to break it up as much as possible so that it doesn't fry as one big ball of garlic. If the garlic bubbles and hisses violently, turn off the heat and leave the oil to cool before attempting to cook in it. Fry the garlic gently for about 3 minutes until it begins to turn golden brown, then remove it from the hot oil using a sieve or kitchen spider and drain on kitchen paper. Use a fork to break up the garlic as it drains and crisps up.

Fry the peanuts in the same oil, but reduce the temperature of the oil to 160°C to give the nuts longer to fry to the core without burning on the outside. Fry the nuts for 6–8 minutes, keeping your eye on them and moving them gently at all times. Nuts in constant contact with the base of the pan will burn, so it is important to keep them moving. When they start to turn golden brown, remove them from the oil and drain on kitchen paper. I change the kitchen paper a few times as the nuts are cooling to ensure they are not greasy.

Place all the remaining ingredients in a large bowl with the peanuts and garlic and use both hands to mix thoroughly. They are now ready to eat.

SALTED TURMERIC
BUTTER ROTI

125g plain flour, sifted

1 teaspoon coriander seeds, toasted and lightly bruised

1 small egg, beaten

100ml warm water

3 tablespoons olive oil, for greasing

150g unsalted butter

15g peeled fresh red turmeric (or 5g dried turmeric)

a sprinkle of coarse sea salt

Rotis were first introduced into Thai cuisine via South Asian immigrants, who borrowed the dish from India. They were cheap to produce and delicious to eat, so they became a common street food. As their popularity continued to rise, so too did the number of roti stalls. Now you can find them being cooked by everyone, everywhere – on the streets, in malls and in homes. This dough can be used for sweet and savoury rotis, so use it however you like – dipped into curries, or just eaten as a snack.

Start by making the roti dough. Place the flour and coriander seeds in a mixing bowl, make a well in the centre, add the egg and rub together until the mixture is the consistency of breadcrumbs. Gradually, add the water and knead for 8–10 minutes. The dough should be tacky but not sticking to the bowl or your fingers. If it's too wet add a little flour; if it's too dry add a little water, but bear in mind that it should be quite wet compared to regular bread dough.

Place the dough in a lightly oiled bowl, and cover with clingfilm; make sure the clingfilm is in direct contact with the dough to stop it crusting over. Leave to rest for a minimum of 30 minutes.

Meanwhile, gently melt the butter in a small frying pan with the turmeric. The clarified (clear) butter will split from the solids, so pour this into a container and discard the turmeric and sediment at the bottom.

Now for the fun bit. If you're feeling ambitious, try the traditional method of slapping out the roti dough. Lightly oil a clean surface, pull off a chunk of dough and roll it into a ball roughly the size of a ping pong ball. Repeat with the rest of the dough. Next, grab a ball and place it on the oiled surface. Flatten it into a rough circular shape, then gently lift the side closest to you and drag it towards you. Lift it quickly but delicately and then slap it back onto the surface (because of the dough's elasticity it doesn't rip too easily and it stretches bigger as you drag it). Repeat this process until the dough is roughly 2–3mm thick (the thinner the better but don't make it too hard to lift into the pan, a few holes are fine). Alternatively, use a rolling pin, or just stretch the dough out with your hands. No one, including myself, gets it perfect first time, so don't worry if it all goes a little pear-shaped, it will still taste amazing.

Heat the clarified butter in a large frying pan over a medium heat (the butter needs to be hot to crisp the dough, but don't burn it). Carefully lift the dough circle into the pan; if it sizzles you're doing it right. Fry for roughly 1 minute on each side until it is golden brown and crispy on both sides. Drain on a tray lined with kitchen paper and sprinkle with coarse sea salt. Repeat.

CRISPY JASMINE RICE CAKES WITH SOY

SERVES 4–5

VE

100ml soy sauce

¼ teaspoon coarse sea salt

500g cooked jasmine rice, still warm

2 litres sunflower oil

At my restaurant, Farang, it's a constant battle to put the correct amount of rice on for the evening, as our customer numbers can be anything from 10 to 500. Inevitably, we often do too much. However, fear not, it never goes to waste and this little snack is one of the ways we put it to use.

Place a sheet of parchment paper on a clean surface. Mix the soy sauce and salt with the warm rice and place in the centre of the parchment. Using both hands, spread it out so that it is about 5cm in depth and as even as you can make it. Spreading out the rice evenly ensures that it all dries at the same time, so make sure there are no clumps. Be light-handed with this process: you do not want to mash the grains together too much as they need as much air flow as possible going through them to aid the drying process. Place another sheet of parchment paper on top and lightly roll over with a rolling pin, keeping the layer of rice as even as possible. Don't compress the grains together too much, but rather aim for it to be 2–3cm in depth.

Carefully lift onto a wire rack and leave the rice in a warm, dry place for about 24 hours, until it has completely dried out (it may be ready a little sooner). Once it is dry snap it into 4cm by 4cm pieces and set aside.

Heat the oil in a large, wide saucepan to 220°C. To check the temperature of the oil, drop in a small piece of rice cake: it should sink to the bottom and then immediately burst with bubbles as the rice grains pop and release air, making it float straight up to the top. If the rice remains at the bottom of the pan, the oil is not hot enough; if it turns black immediately, it is too hot.

These rice cakes do not take long to cook; when they are light in colour and all the rice grains have expanded, carefully remove them using a slotted spoon and drain on kitchen paper. Sprinkle with a little more salt if you like and either eat immediately or store in an airtight container for 1–2 days.

2 tablespoons chopped
coriander roots

8 garlic cloves, peeled

8 green bird's-eye chillies

a pinch of coarse sea salt

2 tablespoons caster sugar

juice of 4 lemons

juice of 2 mandarins
(or clementines)

4 tablespoons fish sauce

4 oysters

100g table salt mixed with
25ml water, to serve

4 physalis, finely sliced

2 kaffir lime leaves, julienned,
to garnish

coriander, finely chopped,
to garnish

GRILLED OYSTERS
WITH SOUR FRUIT,
CHILLI AND LEMON

If you want, you can skip the grilling and eat the oysters fresh. I personally love them either way, so it's up to you. The tip for a good oyster is to prepare it as close to the cooking time as possible. If you have purchased them early, store them flat side up on a layer of ice on a perforated tray and cover with a damp tea towel. This way they will keep cool and won't be submerged in any water.

In a pestle and mortar pound the coriander roots, garlic, then chillies (in that order) to a coarse paste, using the salt as an abrasive. Add the sugar and pound for a few more seconds. This should leave you with a relatively smooth paste, though a little chunk is not the end of the world. Finally, add the lemon and mandarin juices along with the fish sauce. The sauce should taste sweet, salty, sour and hot. Exact quantities are impossible to give, as the strength of the ingredients varies depending on where they are grown, so adjust the seasoning to suit your tastes.

Next, prepare the oysters. Hold one flat-side up. When looking at the oyster, the pointed side is known as the hinge (this is how the oyster holds its shell closed) and it is this part that needs to be prised open. Holding a tea towel in your non-shucking hand to protect from any slips, hold the oyster down tightly and gently ease the shucking knife into the gap in the shell. Once you get the tip of the knife in you'll find you can quite easily shuffle it about to make the gap larger. Use the knife to open the oyster shell like a hinge on a door, but be careful not to spill the brine or damage the oyster. The brine should be clear; if it is not, it is a bad oyster so discard it. Use a spoon to detach the oyster from its shell, then return it to its shell. At this point the oyster can be eaten raw with the dressing, so skip to the last step of this recipe if you want or repeat with the remaining oysters.

Preheat the grill to hot and place the oysters in their shells on the grill pan and grill for 2 minutes on each side.

Serve the oysters on a pile of wet salt with the dressing poured over and the physalis placed on top. If you want to impress, add a sprinkling of coriander and jullienned lime leaves.

CHICKEN SATAY BITES IN BANANA LEAF PARCELS

SERVES 3–4 GF

100ml vegetable oil

250g peanut satay curry paste (see page 160)

1 tablespoon palm sugar (or soft dark brown sugar)

1 tablespoon fish sauce

200ml coconut cream

100ml chicken stock

6 chicken thighs, on the bone

6 40 x 25cm sheets of banana leaves (or tin foil)

1 tablespoon tamarind water

10g Thai sweet basil (or Italian basil), to garnish

10g ginger, peeled and julienned, to garnish

2 spring onions, sliced, to garnish

1 lime, cut into wedges, to serve

When I first started cooking street food in London I was given a pitch right in the middle of the children's play area of Street Feast. Although it's so delicious I have devoted my entire career to the cuisine, spicy Thai food is a tough sell to the little ones, so I created this, which went down a storm. The banana leaves add flavour but, if you can't find them, foil is fine.

Heat the oil to high in a large non-stick frying pan. Add the satay curry paste and fry for 10–12 minutes until the paste darkens slightly and the smell becomes fragrant, using a metal spoon to stir and scrape the paste. Add the palm sugar, reduce the heat to medium, and continue to stir and scrape until the sugar caramelises and the paste darkens further. Add the fish sauce – this will deglaze any paste that has stuck to the pan. Remove from the heat and add 100ml of the coconut cream and two-thirds of the stock, then allow to cool.

Use two-thirds of the paste to marinate the chicken thighs, making sure to coat them thoroughly, and refrigerate the remaining paste for now. Wrap the thighs in the banana leaves: on a flat surface, lay 2 banana leaves on top of each other, then lay a third with the grain of the leaf facing the opposite direction – this will give strength to the parcel. Place 3 chicken thighs in the centre of the banana leaves, and carefully wrap them up from each side to make a rectangular parcel, then use cocktail sticks to secure the corners by weaving them in and out of the leaves. Repeat with the remaining 3 leaves and 3 thighs. This can be tricky, so don't worry if the parcels don't look perfect; the idea is that the meat steams with the paste in the oven, so even if the meat is half wrapped, it should still work fine. Practice makes perfect! Refrigerate the parcels for a minimum of 3 hours, but ideally overnight.

Preheat the oven to 220°C/gas mark 7. Place the parcels on a baking tray and roast for 35–40 minutes. Open up the banana leaves and check that the chicken is cooked and piping hot throughout. Heat the remaining satay curry paste with the remaining stock and coconut cream, add the tamarind water and check the seasoning: it should be sweet and sour with a delicate hit of chilli and salt.

Serve the parcels open in bowls with the extra satay curry paste poured over the top. Sprinkle with the basil, ginger and spring onions, with wedges of lime on the side.

CURRIED SALT AND PEPPER SQUID WITH FRESH LIME

3 teaspoons coriander seeds

I teaspoon black peppercorns

I teaspoon fennel seeds

3 teaspoons cumin seeds

3 teaspoons ground ginger

4 teaspoons ground turmeric

2 teaspoons chilli powder

400g squid, cleaned and scored, roughly chopped into 3cm pieces

I litre sunflower oil

I teaspoon coarse sea salt

10g coriander leaves, chopped, to garnish

I lime, cut into wedges, to serve

Good quality squid is a delicious thing to eat, particularly baby squid, as it's more tender, and is so simple to cook. This recipe takes minutes from start to finish and on a summer's day, sat in the sunshine, I can't think of anything better than Thai calamari.

Start by making the curry powder. In a large frying pan toast the spices. When toasting spices you should always put them over a medium–low heat and toast them according to their size; larger spices first and for longer. In this instance, toast the coriander seeds first followed by the black peppercorns, then the fennel seeds and lastly the cumin. When a spice begins to change colour and release a fragrant smell then it is ready to use. Once toasted, add the ginger, turmeric and chilli powder – these powders will toast in the residual heat from the other spices – then grind everything together to make the curry powder.

Pat the squid pieces dry with kitchen paper to remove all the moisture, then transfer to a bowl and toss through the curry powder.

Heat the oil in a saucepan to about 220°C. Have a tray lined with kitchen paper at the ready and flash-fry the squid for 15–20 seconds, then drain on the tray and sprinkle with the salt. Serve immediately sprinkled with the coriander and with wedges of lime to squeeze over.

TIPS

When removing the skin from squid, it helps to dip your fingers in table salt as this gives you the extra grip needed to peel the skin off with ease. Also, make sure you score the squid with a very sharp knife, aimed at a 75-degree angle to the flesh, and score in one direction across the whole length. Score as deep as half way through the flesh as this ensures it cooks quickly and evenly.

60g palm sugar (or soft dark brown sugar)

80ml fish sauce

60ml thick tamarind water

500g minced pork belly (20% fat content so the sausages are nice and juicy)

2 sticks lemongrass, outer layer removed and sliced as thinly as possible

10g coriander leaves, roughly chopped

8 kaffir lime leaves, stems removed and julienned

100g roasted red curry paste (see page 166)

1 tablespoon table salt

6 red bird's-eye chillies, thinly sliced

20g toasted semi-crushed peanuts

½ Chinese cabbage, leaves separated

RED CURRY SAUSAGE WITH RAW CABBAGE, CHILLI, PEANUTS AND KAFFIR

This is an absolute banger of a dish! Smoky, salty, spicy, sweet and sour – everything a person with a taste for Thai would expect in a meal. The sausage originates from Northern Thailand and traditionally is grilled over charcoal and I have to admit, the added smokiness of cooking these bad boys over an open fire makes a tasty difference. Here, though, I show you how to make them quite simply in the comfort of your home kitchen, just in case you can't be bothered to get the barbecue out.

Begin by making the sausages. In a small saucepan over a medium heat, melt together the palm sugar and fish sauce. When the sugar has melted, remove the pan from the heat, add the tamarind water and leave to cool. In a large mixing bowl pour this over the minced pork belly, add the lemongrass, coriander, kaffir lime leaves and red curry paste, and mix together thoroughly using both hands. When you are happy that all the ingredients are combined, pick up small handfuls of the mixture and throw them into a clean mixing bowl with force. This slaps the proteins of the meat together and ensures the mixture holds together well.

Lay a few layers of clingfilm on a clean surface. Place one-fifth of the sausage mixture in the centre in a rough sausage shape then roll the clingfilm tightly around the pork mince and using both hands continue to roll into a tight sausage shape. Repeat this process four more times until there is no sausage mixture left. Pierce the end of each sausage with a wooden skewer and run it down the entire length through the middle. Leave these skewers to rest in the fridge for at least 30 minutes, but ideally overnight.

Bring a large saucepan of water with the salt to a simmer. Gently drop the sausages into the pan and poach for 4–5 minutes, enough for the sausages to hold their shape then remove the sausages from the water, immediately remove the clingfilm and allow the sausages to drip dry while cooling.

The sausages can be grilled, cooked in the oven, in a pan or gently smoked over a barbecue. Just make sure that they are piping hot throughout before serving. Ideally, they should have a slightly golden–orange colour on the outside from being gently cooked at about 180°C and turned often. Allow to rest for 5 minutes before slicing. Serve the sausages sliced at an angle and spread out over a plate, sprinkled with the chillies and peanuts, with large pieces of cabbage ready for diners to wrap up the sausages with.

CHILLI, PRAWN AND PORK BELLY OMELETTE WITH FRESH HERBS AND CHILLI OIL

1 teaspoon chopped coriander roots

½ teaspoon white peppercorns, toasted

2 garlic cloves, peeled

½ teaspoon coarse sea salt

2 green bird's-eye chillies, sliced

1 tablespoon vegetable oil

100g pork belly, blanched in salted water, skin removed and roughly shredded

4 prawns, heads and tails removed, deveined and sliced in half lengthways

4 large eggs, beaten and left at room temperature for 20 minutes

2 tablespoons smoky chilli oil (see page 155)

a handful of coriander leaves, chopped, to garnish

a handful of Thai sweet basil leaves (or any basil), chopped, to garnish

Breakfast, lunch, dinner – who cares, these babies are great for a feed at any point in the day. I have gone for luxury in this recipe with the surf 'n' turf of pork and prawn, but you can just use one or even skip the meat and fish altogether and just have a chilli omelette with fresh herbs as a quick snack. If you don't like it too hot use just one chilli, and try duck eggs for extra richness.

In a pestle and mortar or food processor pound the coriander roots, white peppercorns, garlic, sea salt and chillies to a coarse paste.

Heat the vegetable oil in a large saucepan and fry the paste. At the same time, add the pork belly and prawns and fry until the prawns are cooked and the garlic and chillies begin to turn golden brown and all the flavours have infused. Add the beaten eggs and tip the pan so that the egg runs to the edge of the pan and the pork belly and prawn mixture becomes part of the omelette. Cook for 2 minutes until the underside of the omelette has turned light brown and is slightly crisp. Now, either carefully flip the omelette over or put the pan under the grill for about a minute until the top is light brown and slightly crisp too. The omelette should be moist in the middle and crispy on either side.

Chop the omelette into bite-sized pieces and place on a serving plate as a sharing snack. Top with the chilli oil and the herbs.

CRAB, SALMON, YELLOW BEAN AND CHIVE CRISPY WONTONS WITH A SOY AND SESAME DIP

2 bird's-eye chillies, roughly chopped

1 tablespoon roughly chopped coriander roots

4 garlic cloves, peeled

20g ginger, peeled and roughly chopped

30g yellow bean sauce

1 tablespoon vegetable oil

2 tablespoons caster sugar

2 tablespoons finely chopped Chinese chives (or other chives)

60g smoked salmon, finely shredded

50g cooked and picked white or brown crab meat

10–15 wonton wrappers

plain flour, for dusting

1 teaspoon sesame oil

100ml soy sauce

½ teaspoon toasted sesame seeds

Wontons are such fun things to play around with as they are great in soups and curries or just steamed, fried or roasted as a snack. Fresh wonton pastry is amazing – and worth getting hold of if you can – but it's often difficult to find, so it's fine to use frozen, which is readily available. Use either white or brown crab meat; both are delicious.

In a pestle and mortar or food processor pound the chillies, coriander roots, garlic, ginger and lastly the yellow bean sauce to a paste.

Heat the oil to high in a large frying pan and fry the paste for 6–8 minutes until the chillies, garlic and ginger have softened and the paste has darkened slightly. Add the sugar and fry for a further minute until the sugar has caramelised and begins to darken, then remove from the heat. Once cooled, add the chives, salmon and crab meat and mix thoroughly.

Lay the wonton wrappers on a lightly floured surface and place a teaspoon of the mixture into the centre of each wrapper. Wet your index finger with water and moisten two edges of the pastry, then fold over the opposite two edges and press together so that they stick to one another, sealing the filling within and leaving you with a triangle-shaped wonton that is fat in the middle. Fold the pointed edges of the triangle around the fat middle so that the wonton stands up on its own. Repeat with the remaining wrappers and filling.

Preheat the oven to 180°C/gas mark 4. Place the wontons on a baking tray lined with parchment paper and bake for 15–20 minutes until they are golden brown and crispy.

Mix the sesame oil with the soy sauce and serve as a dipping sauce alongside the wontons sprinkled with the sesame seeds.

SERVES 3-4

80g palm sugar (or soft light brown sugar)

80ml fish sauce

50ml thick tamarind water

200g salmon, skin and bloodline removed and chopped into small chunks

200g cod, skin and bloodline removed and chopped into small chunks

150g green curry paste (see page 167)

1 egg, beaten

1 litre sunflower oil

2 limes, cut into wedges, to serve

100ml sweet chilli sauce (see page 150), to serve

SALMON AND COD GREEN CURRY BALLS WITH SWEET CHILLI SAUCE

When buying your fish, ask your fishmonger to include a little smoked fish in the mix. This, along with the fresh green curry paste, turns these into little spicy balls of fishy heaven. I use salmon and cod here, but it works with a range of different fish, even prawns, but steer clear of flat fish as the proteins do not break down enough and the texture is not right for this dish.

In a small saucepan, gently melt the palm sugar and fish sauce, making sure not to boil the mixture and caramelise the sugar. Add the tamarind water and set aside to cool.

Put the fish, tamarind fish sauce mixture and green curry paste in a food processor and combine well, then tip out into a mixing bowl and mix in the beaten egg using your hands. If you add the egg to the food processor it will whisk air into it, which will make the cakes float as they fry, cooking them unevenly. Shape the mixture into fish cakes by scooping up 20–30g of the mixture and then flatten it slightly by closing the palm of your hand around it.

Heat the oil in a medium deep saucepan to 180°C. Check the temperature of the oil by placing a fish cake into it. It should bubble gently and take 2–3 minutes to become hot throughout and have a golden brown colour all around with a crisp texture on the outside. If you're happy with the temperature, go ahead and cook the cakes, cooking 5–6 at any one time so that the temperature of the oil doesn't cool down too much. When the cakes are cooked, drain onto kitchen paper.

Serve the cakes immediately with wedges of lime and a spoon of sweet chilli sauce.

GF SERVES 4
AS A SNACK OR SIDE

1 sour eating apple, grated

10g coriander leaves,
roughly torn

10g mint leaves, roughly torn

200g salmon, bloodline
and pin bones removed and
sliced into 1cm thick pieces

10g dill, chopped

FOR THE NAHM JIM

2 tablespoons chopped
coriander roots

8 garlic cloves, peeled

8 green bird's-eye chillies

a pinch of coarse sea salt

2 tablespoons caster sugar

juice of 5 limes

juice of 2 mandarins
(or clementines)

4 tablespoons fish sauce

GREEN NAHM JIM
CURED SALMON
WITH APPLE AND DILL

Amongst Thai chefs, bird's eye chillies are referred to as 'scuds', sensibly nicknamed after the missiles developed by the Soviet Union during the Cold War. So it will come as no surprise that these little beauties can cause some damage if you're not careful – be sure to keep them clear of your eyes and other delicate places. I still remember the first time I got jungle curry paste in my eye; although my colleagues found it hilarious, it's an experience I would not wish on anyone!

First make the *nahm jim*. In a pestle and mortar pound the coriander roots, garlic, then chillies (in that order) to a coarse paste, using the salt as an abrasive, if necessary. Add the sugar and pound for a few more seconds. This should leave you with a relatively smooth paste, though a little chunk is not the end of the world. Finally, add the lime and mandarin juices along with the fish sauce. The sauce should taste sweet, salty, sour and hot. Exact quantities are impossible to give, as the strength of the ingredients varies depending on where they are grown, so adjust the seasoning to suit your tastes.

Divide the *nahm jim* dressing between two large bowls. In one, add the apple, coriander and mint; in the other, place the salmon and gently toss to ensure that all the fish is coated in the dressing. Leave the salmon in the dressing for 1–2 minutes, then remove and gently toss in the apple and mint sauce. Serve on a large plate sprinkled with the dill.

SERVES 2–3

6 garlic cloves, peeled

2 teaspoons chopped coriander roots (optional)

a pinch of coarse sea salt

100ml light soy sauce

½ teaspoon dried chilli powder

1 tablespoon soft brown sugar

60ml olive oil

500g cavolo nero, thick stems removed and discarded, torn into 4 x 8cm pieces

CRISPY CAVOLO NERO
WITH DRIED CHILLI, GARLIC AND SOY

People always say that you have to wait until after the first frost to allow cavolo nero (and kale) to sweeten naturally and be its best. I agree about the sweetness, but to waiting, most certainly not! If your cavolo nero is a bit bitter, stick it in the freezer for 45 minutes, as it will help sweeten and soften the leaves, making them delicious to eat and easier to cook.

In a pestle and mortar or food processor pound the garlic and coriander roots to a paste, using the salt as an abrasive. Add all the remaining ingredients (except the cavolo nero) and loosely combine. Toss this dressing through the cavolo nero, making sure to coat every piece. Set aside the dressing left in the bowl that does not cling to the cavolo nero.

   Preheat the oven to 180°C/gas mark 4. Lay the cavolo nero out on large baking trays, trying not to overlap the leaves too much to allow for even cooking. Place in the oven for about 10 minutes, but check every few minutes until it is crisp and ready to eat. Make sure you check it regularly as if it is left for too long it will turn brown and taste bitter. After a few minutes, your kitchen will begin to fill with the smell of roast garlic – most definitely one of my favourite smells.

   When crispy, drizzle with the reserved dressing, making sure to strain out any raw garlic. Serve immediately.

SOUR FRUITS AND ROASTED CHILLI SALT

SERVES 3-4

GF

VE

2 red bird's-eye chillies,
roughly chopped

I tablespoon caster sugar

I tablespoon coarse sea salt

I teaspoon chilli powder

I guava, I green mango and
I green apple, each peeled,
cored or stoned and sliced
into bite-sized chunks

¼ cucumber, sliced into
rounds

I fennel bulb, core and stems
removed, sliced into bite-
sized chunks

2 sprigs of Thai sweet basil,
to garnish

In Thailand, chilli, salt and sugar are often mixed together and eaten with sour fruits and vegetables. The ones in this recipe are my own personal suggestions, but you can use anything you think would be enhanced by a sweet, salty and spicy kick. It's a snack that lends itself to being set out at a dinner party or placed on a bar to have with drinks.

Pound the chillies to a paste in a pestle and mortar or food processor, then add the sugar, salt and chilli powder, and mix until all the ingredients are evenly distributed. Arrange the prepared fruits and vegetables on a plate with the basil sprigs and serve the chilli salt either on the plate or in a ramekin for people to dip into.

CRISPY SALMON SKINS

SERVES 5-6

GF
OPTIONAL

I tablespoon coarse sea salt

I tablespoon olive oil

I teaspoon chilli powder

½ teaspoon garlic powder

I teaspoon light soy sauce
(fish sauce if gluten free)

I side of salmon skin (roughly
100g), scales removed

I litre sunflower oil (optional)

If you like pork scratchings but want a healthier alternative, these are the snack for you. Try them with dipping sauces, fresh chilli or add to salads for texture and crunch. They can be either fried in oil for quick results or made in the oven.

Preheat the oven to 150°C/gas mark 2. Mix the salt, oil, chilli and garlic powders and soy sauce together, then rub into the salmon skin on both sides. Lay on a grill pan so that it's as flat as possible to ensure even cooking then place on the middle shelf of the oven and roast for 30 minutes. At this point it should be dry and beginning to crisp up. If you're in a hurry, it can be removed and fried in oil. To do this, heat I litre sunflower oil to 180°C and fry the dried skin for 15–20 seconds until it is golden brown, then drain on kitchen paper. Bear in mind that the skin won't crisp up until it has been drained and cooled slightly. Check for seasoning: you may need to add a little more salt.

    If you choose not to fry the skin, leave it in the oven and check it every 5 minutes after the initial 30 minutes. I find that an exact cooking time is impossible to give as it all depends on the product. It will usually take 30–45 minutes to crisp up: when the skin begins to curl at the sides and turns golden brown it is ready. Sprinkle with a little more salt if you like, snap the skin into bite-size pieces and serve in a bowl for people to snack on – it tastes great with a beer.

TIPS

Ask for salmon skin at
a fishmongers or at the
supermarket fish counter.
If you can get it smoked,
even better.

6 garlic cloves, peeled

1 tablespoon roughly chopped coriander roots

¾ teaspoon coarse sea salt

80ml oyster sauce

1 tablespoon fish sauce

1 tablespoon toasted coriander seeds, lightly bruised

300–400g venison loin, trimmed and thinly sliced against the grain into 3 x 3cm pieces ½cm thick

2 litres sunflower oil

HEAVENLY VENISON JERKY

When in season, venison can be as juicy and meaty as beef and should be a regular part of the diet, especially in the UK, as it is very well controlled and sustainably hunted. I've heard hundreds of amazing and wonderful ways to make beef jerky, from drying it in the sunshine, like they do in Thailand, to leaving the meat down wind of an open wood fire for days, as they did in the days of the wild west. This recipe is a twist on classic beef jerky. I've made it as simple as possible so it can easily be made at home. It's perfect eaten with some sour chilli dipping sauce, fresh herbs and crispy garlic, washed down with a beer, or just on its own as a snack.

Pound the garlic and coriander roots to a coarse paste in a pestle and mortar or food processor, using the salt as an abrasive, if necessary. Add the oyster sauce, fish sauce and coriander seeds, and mix thoroughly.

Put the venison in a bowl and add the paste, using your hands to make sure the meat is completely coated in the marinade. Leave to marinate for 1 hour at room temperature.

Place a sheet of parchment paper underneath a wire rack (or any tray that raises the meat off the surface so there is air flow underneath as well as on top). On a clean surface, use a rolling pin to roll out each piece of venison as thinly as you possibly can, rolling the coriander seeds into the meat. Don't worry too much if you make a few rips here and there. Lay the meat out flat onto the parchment paper.

Leave the venison in a warm, dry environment for 24 hours, turning the meat over once to ensure that both sides dry at the same rate. It is ready when you can touch it without any moisture or sauce coming off on your fingers, and it should resemble jerky. The meat can be refrigerated for 3–4 days before cooking or you can cook it straight away.

Heat the oil to 180°C. To test the temperature of the oil, drop a piece of jerky into it. It should take 15–20 seconds to turn crispy and golden brown. Fry the venison jerky a few pieces at a time, then drain on kitchen paper. These are best served straight away.

TEMPURA OYSTERS WITH PICKLED GARLIC AND CHILLI

100g tempura flour

1 teaspoon coarse sea salt

50g rice flour

50g tapioca flour

250ml ice-cold sparkling water

4 fresh oysters

1 litre vegetable oil,

1 long red chilli, thinly sliced, to garnish

4 sprigs coriander, to garnish

1 lime, cut into wedges, to serve

sweet chilli sauce (see page 150), to serve (optional)

FOR THE PICKLED GARLIC

100g caster sugar

100ml distilled white vinegar

1 tablespoon fish sauce

1 head garlic, cloves peeled (ideally young garlic)

This is a quick snack or starter that's really simple to make. Pickled garlic is one of my favourite ingredients and works well with the natural saltiness of the oysters. I have included a quick recipe below but you can also buy it ready made.

Start by making the pickle. In a small saucepan, bring the sugar, vinegar, fish sauce and 100ml water to a simmer, then remove from the heat when the sugar has dissolved. Add the garlic whilst still hot and to allow to infuse. This can be kept in a sterilised and sealed jar in a cool, dry environment indefinitely, or it can be kept sealed in the fridge for 2–3 weeks.

To make the batter, sift the tempura flour into a bowl, add half the salt, half the rice flour and all the tapioca flour. Slowly add 200ml of the sparkling water, stirring with a fork, not a whisk (this will leave a few small lumps in the batter, which add extra texture once fried). The batter should be thick enough to cling to your fingers but loose enough to run off in one motion without dripping. Add a little more sparkling water if needed. Place in the freezer while you prepare the oysters (however, unless you want a batter ice lolly it's best not to get too far ahead with this step!).

Next, shuck the oysters following the instructions on page 26. Once the oyster is open, use a spoon to detach it from the shell, then place to one side. Add the brine to the batter and place the shells in boiling water for 1 minute to clean, then remove and dry for later use.

Meanwhile, heat the oil in a large wide saucepan to 220°C. Sift the remaining rice flour onto a tray and add the oysters, making sure that each is coated with a layer of the flour. Use a little more flour if needed, but be careful to only give a light coating. Now check the temperature of the oil by dropping in a little cold batter. If it bubbles for 30 seconds and turns light golden brown, you're good to go. Use chopsticks or tongs to dip the oysters into the batter and then carefully drop into the hot oil. Cook for about a minute, turning half way, then drain on kitchen paper and sprinkle with the remaining salt. It's best to cook only 2 oysters at a time to ensure that they cook evenly and that the oil temperature doesn't cool down too much.

To serve, place the oysters back in their shells and top each one with sliced pickled garlic, chopped chilli and coriander sprigs, with a wedge of lime on the side to squeeze over. These oysters are also great eaten with sweet chilli as a dipping sauce.

200g tempura flour

I teaspoon table salt

200g rice flour

50g tapioca flour

50g oats

550ml ice-cold sparkling water

2 litres sunflower oil

I tablespoon dried turmeric

400g squid, cleaned, scored and chopped into bite-sized pieces

½ teaspoon coarse sea salt

80ml burnt chilli dipping sauce (see page 146), to serve

I lime, cut into wedges, to serve

sweet chilli sauce (see page 150), to serve (optional)

LIGHTLY SPICED OAT TEMPURA SQUID
WITH BURNT CHILLI DIPPING SAUCE

The secret to making a good tempura is to have cold batter and hot oil. As the cold batter hits the hot oil it bounces out at the same time as it cooks, creating air bubbles. This is where the crunch comes from. Using sparkling water adds to the air bubbles, resulting in a seriously crunchy tempura.

Start by making the batter. In a bowl, sift the tempura flour, table salt, 100g of the rice flour and the tapioca flour together. Add the oats and slowly add 500ml of the sparkling water, stirring the batter with a fork, not a whisk (this will leave a few small lumps in the batter which add extra texture once fried; if a whisk were to be used, it would make a completely smooth batter). The batter should be thick enough to cling to your fingers but loose enough run off in one motion without dripping. Add a little more sparkling water if needed. Place the batter in the freezer while you prepare the remaining ingredients (however, unless you want a batter ice lolly it's best not to get too far ahead with this step!).

Meanwhile, heat the oil in a large, wide saucepan to about 220°C. Sift the remaining rice flour together with the turmeric into a tray and add the squid, making sure it is thoroughly coated in the turmeric flour mixture. Check the temperature of the oil by dropping a little cold batter into it: if it bubbles for 30 seconds and turns light golden brown, you're good to go. Using chopsticks or tongs, dip pieces of squid into the batter and then drop them into the hot oil. Cook the pieces for 30–40 seconds, then drain on kitchen paper and sprinkle with the sea salt. It's probably best to work with 5 or 6 pieces at a time to ensure that they cook evenly and that the oil temperature does not cool down too much.

Serve the squid in a big pile with burnt chilli dipping sauce to share and wedges of lime to squeeze over. These also taste great with sweet chilli sauce.

STEAMED SMOKED TROUT

4 duck eggs, whisked for
1 minute so they begin
to turn pale

1 tablespoon fish sauce

1 teaspoon caster sugar

2 long red chillies,
thinly sliced

5g ginger, peeled and
fine julienned

300g smoked trout, shredded
into bite-sized chunks

100ml thick coconut cream

½ teaspoon white
peppercorns

½ teaspoon dried turmeric

8 Thai shallots, thinly sliced
(or 2 banana shallots), plus
a little extra to garnish

2 tablespoons Chinese chives,
roughly chopped (or other
chives), plus a little extra
to garnish

10g Thai sweet basil,
shredded (or other basil),
plus a little extra to garnish

Essentially, these are little fishy steamed omelettes and are delicious served as a starter – light, delicate and packed full of flavour. I've used trout (because I love it!), but salmon, haddock, prawns and even smoked mussels would work equally well.

Add all the ingredients to a mixing bowl and mix well. Divide evenly between 4 ramekins or small bowls and wrap them in clingfilm. Meanwhile, heat a steamer, then put all four bowls in the steamer and cook for 2–3 minutes until the egg has cooked and the mixture is hot throughout.

Remove the ramekins from the steamer and discard the clingfilm. Serve immediately, topped with a few fresh sliced Thai shallots, Chinese chives and basil.

FRIED *AND* SALTED PRAWN HEADS *WITH* SWEET CHILLI

SERVES 2-3

GF
OPTIONAL

15–20 prawn heads
(young, smaller prawns
are best)

200ml light soy sauce
(fish sauce if gluten free)

200g rice flour (or plain
flour), sifted

1 litre sunflower oil

½ teaspoon coarse sea salt

½ teaspoon caster sugar

100ml sweet chilli sauce
(see page 150), to serve
(optional)

1 lime, cut into wedges,
to serve

Prawn heads are an absolute wonder product and are used across Asia in a range of different ways. In Thailand, the brains (known as *tamale*) are valued for their intense earthy, shrimpy flavour, which can be used to add depth to sauces, curries and soups. A chef I used to work with always used to say 'fry it before you bin it'. To be honest, most of the time I do not listen to words of wisdom like this, but with this recipe he was right.

Soak the prawn heads in the soy sauce for a minimum of 1 hour, though overnight is best. Remove the prawn heads from the soy sauce and toss them in the flour, coating them evenly in a thin layer.

Meanwhile, heat the oil to about 180°C. To test the temperature of the oil, drop in just one head: it should bubble and float without hissing or smoking. Add the prawn heads a few at a time, being sure not to splash hot oil everywhere. Fry for 30–40 seconds, removing them with a slotted spoon as they become golden brown. Drain on kitchen paper and sprinkle with the salt and sugar.

Eat immediately. They should be crunchy and packed full of flavour. They are tasty on their own or served with a sweet chilli sauce and wedges of lime to take them to the next level.

2 STIR-FRIES &LITTLE THINGS

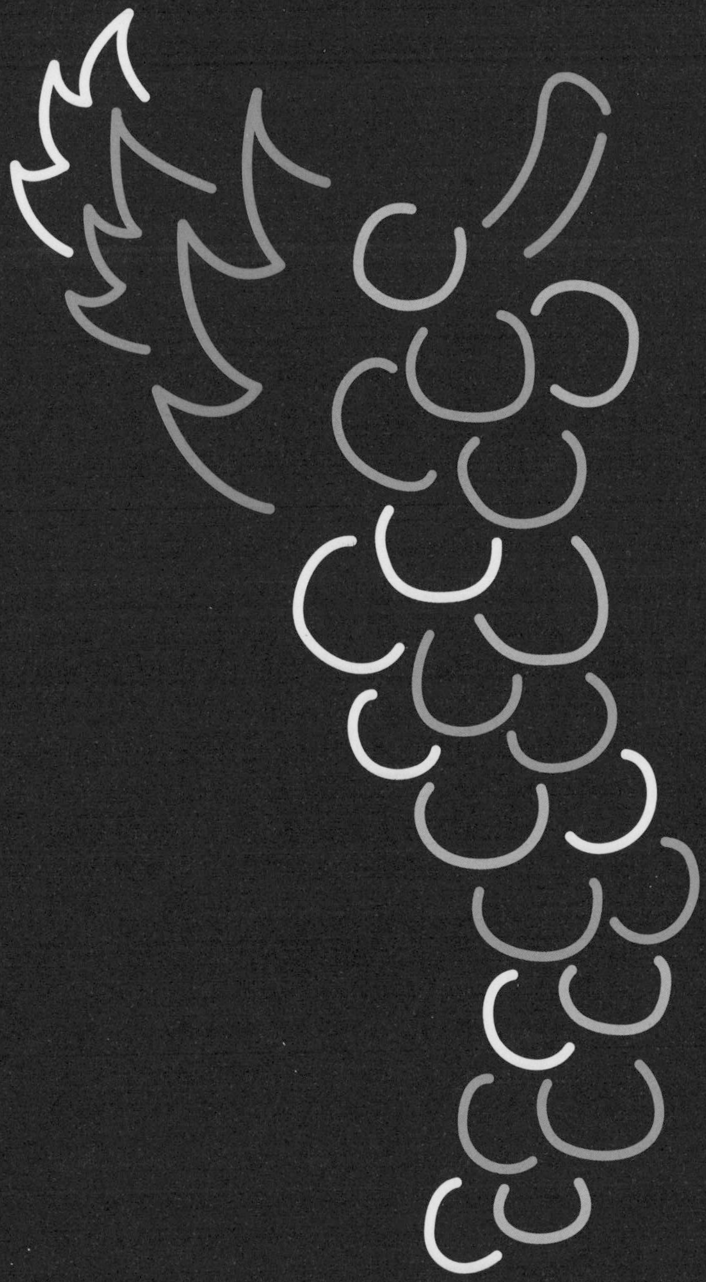

300g pork belly,
skin removed

150g pumpkin, peeled and
chopped into 2cm cubes

5g coarse sea salt

300g palm sugar
(or soft dark brown sugar)

100ml oyster sauce

50ml dark soy sauce

1 pandan leaf, tied in
a knot and torn to release
its flavour (optional)

4cm piece of cassia bark
(or 1 cinnamon stick)

1 star anise

2 fresh bay leaves

100ml fish sauce (depends on
pork fat content and taste)

500ml sunflower oil

4 banana shallots,
thinly sliced

2 spring onions, thinly sliced,
to garnish

green papaya salad,
to serve (optional)

thai sticky rice,
to serve (optional)

STICKY PORK BELLY WITH SALTED ROAST PUMPKIN AND CRISPY SHALLOTS

Ever since I tasted sticky pork for the first time at The Begging Bowl it has become one of my favourite things. Its rich, sweet, salty yet savoury flavours make it the perfect dish to impress friends. In Thailand, it is often eaten with rice and green papaya salad, but it's great just as it is.

In two separate saucepans, bring some salted water to the boil. When boiling, reduce the heat to a simmer and drop the whole pork belly into one pan and the pumpkin pieces into the other. Cook the pumpkin for 4–5 minutes, then refresh under cold running water. It should be soft but not mushy, and still firm and holding its shape. Sprinkle the pumpkin with the salt. Cook the pork belly for 12–15 minutes, making sure the water does not come to a boil – the slower it cooks the more tender it will be. Remove the pork from the pan and set it aside to cool slightly, then chop it into 2cm chunks. Preheat the oven to 160°C/gas mark 3.

Next, make the sauce. In a separate ovenproof dish, add the palm sugar, oyster sauce, soy sauce, pandan leaf, cassia bark, star anise, bay leaves and 50ml of the fish sauce. Heat gently and when the sugar has melted, add the pork belly and stir well, making sure to coat all the pork in the sauce. Place some parchment paper over the top of the pork mixture and transfer to the oven for 30 minutes. Remove the dish from the oven and delicately fold the pumpkin into the mixture, making sure not to mash up any pork or pumpkin as they will both be tender and soft due to the cooking process. Return to the oven for a further 10–15 minutes. The pork should be slightly caramelised and tender, and the pumpkin should be soft.

Meanwhile, heat the oil to about 180°C in a medium saucepan over a high heat. To test the temperature, drop a piece of shallot into the oil: it should bubble and fizz in a controlled manner; if it hisses, then the oil is too hot, so turn off the heat and allow the oil to cool for a few minutes before trying again. Fry the shallots until they begin to turn golden brown, then remove and drain on kitchen paper. Use a fork to pick apart the shallots. They will crisp up nicely as they cool.

Serve the sticky caramelised pork and pumpkin straight out of the oven, topped with the spring onions and crispy shallots. Serve immediately and, as suggested in the introduction, with a salad and some Thai sticky rice for mopping up all the rich juices.

30ml vegetable oil

2 skinless chicken breasts,
roughly chopped

20g green beans, topped,
tailed and cut in half

4 kaffir lime leaves, torn

100ml chicken stock

50g crispy chilli and
coconut jam (see page 161)

100ml coconut cream

1 teaspoon caster sugar

1 tablespoon fish sauce

6–8 white peppercorns,
ground

10g Thai sweet basil
(or Italian basil)

10g coriander, chopped

10g chives, chopped into
3cm pieces

steamed jasmine rice,
(optional)

STIR-FRIED CHICKEN, COCONUT AND CHILLI JAM WITH VEGETABLES

When I have a crazy week, this dish is my absolute favourite, as it can be made in minutes as long as you have the chilli jam made already. My advice is, make a big batch of the chilli jam (see page 161) and have it waiting for you in the fridge. Another thing that makes it a winner is you can serve the same salad with different meats, fish and vegetables – it's great with prawns, salmon and baby corn – so try this recipe first to get a feel for the flavour combinations, then get creative yourself.

Heat the oil in a wok. When smoking hot, throw in the chicken and stir-fry until lightly coloured. Add the green beans and lime leaves and toss in the juices, then add the chicken stock. Once hot, add the chilli jam: this will create a thick, flavoursome sauce that coats the chicken and beans. Add the coconut cream, sugar, fish sauce and white pepper, then remove from the heat.

Now add the the cold ingredients. Toss through the basil, coriander and chives, then place on a plate so they wilt slightly in the residual heat from the stir-fry. If you have it left over from making the chilli jam, garnish with a sprinkling of crispy garlic or shallots (or both). This dish is great accompanied with steamed jasmine rice or just eaten as it is, straight from the wok.

500ml vegetable stock

I fresh bay leaf

¼ teaspoon white peppercorns

I star anise

4cm piece cassia bark (or I cinnamon stick)

50ml light soy sauce

½ teaspoon coarse sea salt

1–2 teaspoons caster sugar

2 red bird's-eye chillies, bruised

I pak choi, core removed and leaves cut into bite-sized chunks (or cabbage)

I teaspoon goji berries

¼ large cucumber, peeled and sliced into rounds

30g (a couple of slices) daikon (mooli)

10 Thai shallots, peeled and bruised in a mortar

500ml sunflower oil

6 garlic cloves, peeled

10g Thai sweet basil, roughly torn

100g fine vermicelli rice noodles, blanched in boiling salted water for I minute, then refreshed under cold water

CLEAR VERMICELLI NOODLE SOUP
WITH FRESH HERBS AND GOJI BERRIES

This soup has a light broth and can easily be whipped up for a quick lunch. I have also served it with steamed jasmine rice, rather than noodles, which turns it into a *congee* type dish, perfect eaten in the late morning brunch. For me, there is something medicinal about this soup; I always crave it when I'm ill and feel better afterwards. It's also delicious with fresh prawns and poached chicken.

Heat the stock in a medium saucepan to a simmer. Using a square of muslin or thin cloth, tie the bay leaf, white peppercorns, star anise and cassia bark together in a bouquet garni and add to the stock with the soy sauce, salt and I teaspoon of the sugar.

When the liquid begins to bubble, drop in the chillies, pak choi, goji berries, cucumber, daikon and Thai shallots, and reduce the heat to low to slowly soften the vegetables and fruit. Simmer for 6–8 minutes until softened and the cucumber has gone a little soft like pickled gherkin. Taste for seasoning: the soup should be sweet and savoury, so adjust it to suit your palate.

Meanwhile, heat the oil in a small saucepan to about 180°C. Pound the garlic to a coarse paste in a pestle and mortar, then drop it into the oil, using a fork to stop the garlic clumping together. Fry for 1–2 minutes until the garlic begins to turn golden brown, then remove and place it onto kitchen paper to drain and crisp up.

Stir the basil into the hot soup and serve on top of the cooked noodles; the heat of the broth will heat the noodles to a comfortable eating temperature. Sprinkle with the fried garlic.

POACHED CHICKEN, SQUASH, COCONUT AND GALANGAL SOUP

50g butternut squash, peeled and sliced into 2 x 2cm pieces (or pumpkin)

200ml chicken or vegetable stock

300ml coconut cream

2–3 tablespoons fish sauce (or soy sauce)

½ teaspoon coarse sea salt

10g galangal, peeled and cut into 2cm pieces and bruised in a mortar

2 coriander roots (5g), bruised

2 green bird's-eye chillies, bruised

2 sticks lemongrass, cut into 2cm pieces and bruised

2 kaffir lime leaves, torn

8 Thai shallots, peeled and slightly bruised

1 chicken breast, skin and fat removed, sliced into 2 x 2cm pieces (optional)

juice of 1 lime

10g Thai sweet basil (or Italian basil), roughly torn

Known as *tom kha gai*, this soup is another absolute classic. I personally think that it's a brilliant winter soup and always like to serve it with some salted squash or pumpkin. It's delicious eaten just as a soup, with rice or with noodles, so go nuts.

Bring a little water to the boil in a small saucepan and drop in the squash. Reduce the heat to a simmer and cook for 3–4 minutes until soft but not quite cooked, then remove from the heat and set aside for a few minutes (you can leave the squash in the water as it will be used immediately).

Put the chicken stock, 100ml of the coconut cream, 2 tablespoons of the fish sauce, the salt, galangal, coriander roots, chillies, lemongrass, kaffir lime leaves, squash (removed from its cooking water) and Thai shallots into a medium saucepan and bring to a simmer. Add the chicken pieces and cook for 4–5 minutes until the chicken is cooked through and the vegetables have softened.

Add the remaining coconut cream, lime juice and the basil, stir and dish out into bowls. Check the seasoning: it should be creamy, salty, a little spicy and aromatic, with a fresh hint of lime.

GREEN PAPAYA, POMEGRANATE AND TIGER PRAWN GLASS NOODLE SALAD

juice of 2 limes

2 teaspoons chilli powder

juice of 1 clementine

2 teaspoons fish sauce

½ teaspoon caster sugar

2 tablespoons table salt

6 tiger prawns, shells removed and deveined

1 green papaya, peeled and shredded, core and pips discarded

150g glass noodles (mung bean noodles), soaked in boiling water for 5 minutes until translucent, then chilled

seeds of 1 pomegranate

10g mint leaves, torn

10g coriander

10g Thai sweet basil

10g *pak chi farang* (Thai long-leaf coriander), chopped (optional)

6 Thai shallots, sliced

Thai people often eat unripe fruits as if they were vegetables, which allows for a range of delicious sweet, bitter and sour flavours. This is a very simple and tasty salad that uses green papaya for its crunchy texture and sweet bitterness. In Thailand, I have seen people prepare a green papaya by peeling it and then holding it with one hand, whilst banging it lengthways with a large sharp knife, producing large uneven shreds of papaya, perfect for salads. If you're not so confident with a knife, it is easiest to use a julienne shredder.

In a small bowl, mix the lime juice, chilli powder, clementine juice, fish sauce and caster sugar. Taste for seasoning: it should be sweet, salty, sour and spicy.

Heat a small saucepan of water with the salt to a medium heat. Drop in the prawns and cook for 1–1½ minutes until they are pink and hot throughout, then remove and toss them into the dressing.

Add all the other ingredients to the bowl and mix well, being careful not to pull the prawns apart. Serve immediately in bowls with chopsticks.

SERVES 4
AS A SNACK OR SIDE

2 fennel bulbs, cores
removed and cut into
2cm strips

3 tablespoons vegetable oil

I tablespoon sesame oil

8 physalis, leaves removed
and cut into quarters

I star fruit, cut into
rough chunks

10g mint leaves, roughly torn

10g coriander leaves, torn

10g Thai sweet basil
(or Italian basil), torn

200g fresh salmon, bloodline
and pin bones removed and
sliced into 1cm thick pieces

FOR THE NAM YUM

2 tablespoons chopped
coriander roots

5 garlic cloves, peeled

4 long red chillies, deseeded
and roughly chopped

a pinch of coarse sea salt,
plus I teaspoon

2 tablespoons caster sugar

juice of 5 limes

juice of I mandarin
(or clementine)

3 tablespoons fish sauce

CURED SALMON WITH RED CHILLI AND GARLIC DRESSING, SOUR FRUITS AND FENNEL

The dressing here is known as *nam yum* and its heavy lime and fish sauce content make it ideal for curing fish. This, alongside sesame-roasted fennel, is a winning combination. Instead of star fruit, you can use any sour fruit such as green apple, green mango or physallis.

First make the dressing. Pound the coriander roots, garlic, then chillies (in that order) to a coarse paste in a pestle and mortar, using the salt as an abrasive. Add the sugar and pound for a few more seconds. This should leave you with a relatively smooth paste, though a little chunk is not the end of the world. Add the lime and mandarin juices and the fish sauce. The sauce should taste sweet, salty, sour and hot. Exact quantities are impossible to give, as the strength of the ingredients varies depending on where they are grown, so adjust the seasoning to suit your tastes.

Preheat the oven to 180°C/gas mark 4. Coat the fennel in the vegetable and sesame oils, then sprinkle with the remaining salt. Roast for 20–25 minutes to slightly char and soften the fennel, then remove from the oven.

Divide the dressing between two large bowls. Place the sour fruits and herbs in one bowl; the salmon in the other, and gently toss to ensure it is evenly coated in the dressing. Leave the salmon in the dressing for 1–2 minutes, then remove and gently add to the rest of the salad in the other bowl. Serve on top of the roasted fennel.

MINCED PORK BELLY, CHILLI, WILD GINGER AND SOY WITH WOK-FRIED EGG

4 red bird's-eye chillies, stems removed (use 2 if you don't like things too hot)

1 tablespoon chopped coriander roots, (optional)

6 garlic cloves, peeled

20g ginger, peeled and roughly chopped

1 teaspoon coarse sea salt

150–200ml vegetable oil

2 large eggs

250g pork belly mince

1 heaped teaspoon caster sugar

2 tablespoons oyster sauce

1 tablespoon soy sauce

10g coriander leaves, torn

10g mint leaves, torn in half

10g Thai sweet basil (or Italian basil), torn

8 Thai shallots, peeled and sliced (or banana shallots)

30g cherry tomatoes, crushed

juice of 1 lime

1 lime, cut into wedges, to serve

steamed jasmine rice, to serve (optional)

The secret to a good stir-fry lies in the preparation. If the ingredients are organised then the cooking takes only minutes. This dish is a perfect example. It's a delicious lunch snack and uses the runny yolk of a wok-fried egg to contribute a rich element to the salad, leaving a sweet, salty, sour and spicy plateful. If you fancy a little more of a fill, it's delicious served with steamed jasmine rice.

Pound the chillies, coriander roots, garlic and ginger to a paste in a pestle and mortar or food processor, using the salt as an abrasive to help combine the ingredients.

The best way to set yourself up for cooking this dish is to separate all the prepared ingredients into bowls and place them within arm's length of the cooker for easy access while cooking. The eggs will cook quickly, so crack them into two separate bowls for convenience and have a plate lined with kitchen paper handy to put them on.

Heat the oil in a large wok to a high heat. When the oil is sizzling, carefully pour in one of the eggs; be careful of splattering oil as it hits the wok. As soon as the egg touches the oil it will begin to cook very fast. Leave it for about 10 seconds, then gently unstick it from the wok, being careful not to split the egg yolk. When the egg white is cooked and the yolk still looks runny (about 20–30 seconds), remove the egg using a slotted wok spoon and place it on the draining plate. Repeat with the second egg.

In the same oil, add the paste you made earlier and stir constantly until golden brown. In the afterheat of frying the eggs this will not take long, so be careful not to burn the paste. To this, add the pork belly mince and continue to fry until the pork is crispy. Add the caster sugar, oyster sauce and soy sauce, and cook for a further minute until the mixture darkens and caramelises. Then add the coriander, mint, basil, Thai shallots, tomatoes and lime juice and toss together.

Serve the stir-fry on a plate with the egg on top and a wedge of lime on the side to squeeze over.

STIR-FRIED SQUID, TURMERIC, GARLIC AND COCONUT CREAM WITH SWEET BASIL AND GREEN PEPPERCORNS

SERVES 2

3 red bird's-eye chillies, roughly chopped

4 garlic cloves, peeled

2 teaspoons whole red turmeric, peeled, sliced and cut into chunks

½ teaspoon coarse sea salt

2 tablespoons vegetable oil

60–80g fresh squid, cleaned and scored

5g fresh green peppercorns

50ml chicken stock

80ml coconut cream

2 tablespoons soy sauce

I teaspoon soft brown sugar

10g Thai sweet basil (or Italian basil), torn

I lime, cut into wedges, to serve

steamed jamine rice, to serve (optional)

Once the ingredients are in front of you, the dish can be ready in minutes. That's the beauty of the wok. If you know you're going to be feeding people, and won't want to be bothered once they've arrived (or will be enjoying the party) all ingredients can be pre-prepared, ready to be tossed through the wok to make things instantly delicious.

Pound the chillies, garlic and turmeric to a paste in a pestle and mortar or food processor, using the salt as an abrasive to help combine the ingredients.

Heat the oil in a wok, then add the paste and cook, stirring constantly to ensure it doesn't stick to the pan. After a minute or so, when the paste starts to turn golden brown, add the squid and green peppercorns and continue to stir and scrape for a further 30 seconds. The squid should firm up quite quickly and begin to curl a little.

Deglaze the wok with the chicken stock, coconut cream, soy sauce and sugar, then add the basil. Serve immediately with wedges of lime. If you want a larger feed, this is awesome with steamed jasmine rice.

TIPS

When preparing squid, dip the ends of your fingers in a little table salt. This will act as an abrasive and help pull off the skin. Or you could just get your fishmonger to do it for you.

As we're flash frying here, I prefer to use baby squid.

STIR FRIES AND LITTLE THINGS

5 long red chillies, deseeded and roughly chopped

4 garlic cloves, peeled

1 tablespoon chopped coriander roots

10g fresh red turmeric, peeled and roughly chopped (or 1 teaspoon dried turmeric)

10g wild ginger (*krachai*), peeled and roughly chopped (or regular ginger)

½ teaspoon coarse sea salt

2 tablespoons vegetable oil

5g green peppercorns, scraped off the stem

2 tablespoons fish sauce

100ml hot fish stock

150ml coconut cream

500g mussels, cleaned and barnacles removed

100g prawns, peeled, deveined and roughly minced

1 tablespoon thick tamarind water

10g Thai sweet basil, torn

4 spring onions, thinly sliced

8 Thai shallots, peeled and sliced

1 lime, cut into wedges, to serve

CHILLI AND RED TURMERIC MUSSELS WITH WILD GINGER, MINCED PRAWNS AND GREEN PEPPERCORNS

This is a wok full of all my favourite things; a perfect dish to crack out on a sunny day in the garden with a bottle of wine. Using a wok is ideal for cooking mussels, as the bowl shape allows them to be adequately submerged in the sauce so that when the lid goes on to steam, they only take around 2 minutes to cook perfectly.

Start by making the paste. Pound the chillies, garlic, coriander roots, turmeric and ginger in a pestle and mortar, using the salt as an abrasive.

Heat the oil in a hot wok and then add the paste, scraping and stirring for about 1 minute until it begins to turn golden brown. Add the green peppercorns and stir-fry for 20 seconds to release their flavour, then deglaze the wok with the fish sauce, fish stock and half the coconut cream. Stir well and add the mussels and minced prawns, giving the wok a gentle toss and being careful not to damage any mussel shells. Cover with a lid and steam for 2 minutes, then remove the lid and gently shake the wok. The mussels should have popped open (discard any that remain closed) and the prawns should be pink and hot throughout.

Add the tamarind water, basil, spring onions, Thai shallots and the remaining coconut cream, then gently stir all the ingredients together. The sauce should be creamy, fishy and savoury, with a mild chilli kick. Serve with lime wedges to squeeze over the top and finger bowls to the ready.

STIR FRIES AND LITTLE THINGS

TIPS

Fresh peppercorns can be found in most Asian supermarkets with a fresh vegetable section. If you can't find them, they can be replaced with half a teaspoon of ground white pepper.

DUCK NOODLE SOUP
WITH GOJI BERRIES, MOOLI, SOY AND PAK CHOI

700ml chicken stock

4 banana shallots, peeled and sliced in half lengthways

1 stick lemongrass, bruised

30g dried goji berries

1 fresh bay leaf, torn

1 star anise

2 x 2cm sticks of cassia bark (or 1 cinnamon stick)

150g mooli, peeled and sliced into 2mm thick rounds

1 large pak choi, core removed and cut into 3cm pieces

1 tablespoon palm sugar (or soft brown sugar)

2 tablespoons light soy sauce

1 tablespoon oyster sauce

2 tablespoons fish sauce

3 tablespoons vegetable oil

3 duck breasts, lightly scored across the skin

150g fine vermicelli rice noodles, blanched for 1 minute, then refreshed under cold water

2 spring onions, thinly sliced, to garnish

10g coriander, chopped, to garnish

1 red bird's-eye chilli, finely sliced, to garnish (optional)

When you are in need of something quick, simple and comforting, this awesome soup will sort you right out. Goji berries have been used in Chinese medicine for centuries, as they are said to boost the immune system and protect against many cancers and heart diseases. They're also packed full of vitamins and antioxidants, so even if you don't have time to make the soup, be sure to neck a few goji berries. When scoring the duck, make sure you don't cut through to the flesh.

In a large saucepan, add the stock, shallots, lemongrass, goji berries, bay leaf, star anise, cassia bark, mooli, pak choi, palm sugar, soy sauce, oyster sauce and fish sauce and slowly bring to a simmer. Cook for 8–10 minutes until the mooli and pak choi are softened, then check seasoning: the soup should be sweet, salty and aromatic. Add a little more fish sauce or sugar if you think it's needed.

Meanwhile, heat the oil in a large frying pan on a medium–high heat and fry the duck breasts skin-side down for 5–6 minutes to allow the skin to crisp up, making sure that the breasts have an even golden brown crisp to the skin. Flip the breasts over and cook the other side for a few minutes, then take the pan off the heat and allow the duck to rest for 5–6 minutes. Slice the duck into ½cm slices. The breast should be nice and pink in the middle with a crispy golden brown skin.

Divide the blanched noodles between three bowls and place a sliced duck breast on each pile of noodles. Carefully pour the soup over the top until the bowl is adequately full, scooping out a few pieces of pak choi and mooli into each bowl. Serve topped with the spring onions and coriander. If you like a little spice, add a few slices of bird's-eye chillies on top for an extra kick.

MINCED CHICKEN AND PRAWN LARB WITH HERBS, ROASTED RICE AND BABY GEM LETTUCE

Larb is a spicy minced meat salad with fresh herbs and usually a hefty amount of chillies. It originates from Lao and is most commonly eaten in the Isaan region of Thailand, which is heavily populated by those of Laos ethnicity. After trying a few recipes in this book you'll probably notice how inventive the Thais are with the food that they create. The backbone of their food stems from a range of cultures which they have then made their own in an incredible way. This simple and unique salad demonstrates this perfectly.

Pound the chillies, garlic, ginger and coriander roots to a paste in a pestle and mortar or food processor, using the salt as an abrasive to help combine the ingredients.

Preheat the oven to 180°C/gas mark 4. Place the jasmine rice on a baking tray and roast for 35–40 minutes until the rice is golden brown, then allow to cool and pound to a fine powder in a pestle and mortar. Make sure it is as fine as possible or it will not be pleasant to eat; the rice should add a little texture to an otherwise soft dish.

Meanwhile, heat the oil in a large wok to a high heat. Add the ginger, garlic and chilli paste, and stir constantly until golden brown. Add the minced chicken and prawns, and fry for 6–8 minutes until they are cooked and hot throughout. Add the palm sugar and cook for a further minute until the mixture darkens and caramelises. Then add the coriander, tamarind, mint, basil, Thai shallots, pak chi farang, apple aubergines, roasted chillies, fish sauce and lime juice, and toss together and taste for seasoning. The salad should be salty, sour and hot.

Serve the *larb* on plates with the lettuce leaves and lime wedges on the side and top the salad with the roasted rice. Delicious on its own or with sticky glutinous rice.

Ingredients

4 red bird's-eye chillies, stems removed

6 garlic cloves, peeled

20g ginger, peeled and roughly chopped

1 tablespoon chopped coriander roots

½ teaspoon coarse sea salt

4 tablespoons jasmine rice

3 tablespoons vegetable oil

100g minced chicken

100g prawns, shells and heads removed, deveined and minced

1 teaspoon palm sugar

10g coriander leaves

1 tablespoon thick tamarind water

10g mint leaves, torn in half

10g Thai sweet basil (or Italian basil), torn

8 Thai shallots, peeled and sliced (or banana shallots)

10 *pak chi farang* (Thai flat-leaf coriander), (optional)

2 apple aubergines, chopped into 6 pieces (optional)

1 tablespoon whole long red chillies, toasted in a dry pan until crispy and charred, then crushed

2 tablespoons fish sauce

juice of 1 lime

1 baby gem lettuce, core removed and leaves separated, to serve

1 lime, cut into wedges, to serve

sticky glutinous rice, to serve (optional)

STIR FRIES AND LITTLE THINGS

100g palm sugar

100ml thick tamarind water

30ml vegetable oil

10 Thai shallots, peeled and thickly sliced (or banana shallots)

6 prawns, shells removed and deveined

1 teaspoon dried shrimp

2 tablespoons (15–20g) brown crab meat

2 medium eggs, beaten

150g flat vermicelli rice noodles (5mm thick), soaked for at least 2 hours in cold water

2–3 tablespoons fish sauce

10g Chinese chives (or other chives), chopped

2 teaspoons smoked chilli powder

20g fresh tofu, fried in a little vegetable oil until golden brown and crispy on the outside and soft on the inside

10g toasted peanuts, lightly crushed

1 tablespoon pickled garlic, thinly sliced (optional)

10g beansprouts

10g coriander, chopped, to ganish

50ml chilli oil (see page 155)

1 lime, cut into wedges, to serve

CRAB AND SHRIMP PAD THAI WITH CHILLI OIL

Pad Thai **probably isn't Thai. The Thai authorities popularised it in the 1930s and 40s in an attempt, at a time of economic suffering, to supply the country with a cheap, healthy, affordable meal. Noodle stir fries are quintessentially Chinese, in fact even** *The Bangkok Post* **has admitted that the only Thai ingredient is the chilli powder. Despite this, it has long since become a very popular Thai dish. In my version, I like to use brown crab meat (***tamale*** in Thai) and melt it around the prawns with a few dried shrimp for a luxurious taste of the sea. However, you can just use a few prawns if you want to save some pennies.**

The trick with a *pad Thai* is to have all the ingredients with arm's reach of a hot wok. The only thing that needs preparing in advance is the tamarind sugar: in a small saucepan on a medium heat, gently melt the palm sugar in the tamarind water, stirring constantly until there are no lumps left. Set aside with all the other ingredients.

Heat the oil in a large wok on a high heat and add the Thai shallots, prawns and dried shrimp. Toss until the prawns are almost cooked and the shallots begin to turn golden brown. Add the brown crab meat and toss a few times; it should mostly melt into the sizzling oil and coat the prawns. Add the eggs and scramble for 30 seconds. Immediately after this, add the noodles, making sure not to add too much of the soaking water to the wok. Stir-fry the noodles by stirring them constantly so that they don't stick to the bottom of the wok. Spread them across the surface of the wok as much as possible to ensure even cooking. They are ready for the next stage when they begin to turn translucent.

Add two-thirds of the tamarind sugar to the wok and pour it around the sides; this ensures that it comes into direct contact with the heat from the wok and caramelises as it dribbles down into the noodles. Toss the noodles in the sauce; the noodles should be dark brown, with no black bits. If they look too light, then add the rest of the tamarind sugar in the same way.

Reduce the heat and add 2 tablespoons of the fish sauce, the Chinese chives, 1 teaspoon of the chilli powder, the tofu, half the peanuts, the pickled garlic and beansprouts, and toss all the ingredients through to warm. Check for seasoning: the dish should be sweet, fishy and savoury, with a smoky chilli kick. If it's too sweet, add the remaining tablespoon of fish sauce.

Sprinkle the noodles with the coriander and serve on a large plate with the remaining peanuts and chilli powder, the chilli oil and lime wedges on the side.

CRISPY PORK BELLY BACON, EGG-FRIED RICE AND BURNT CHILLI SAUCE

150g pork belly, skin removed

4 tablespoons table salt

1 tablespoon cassia bark (or ground cinnamon), toasted

3 fresh bay leaves

1 tablespoon coriander seeds, toasted

1 tablespoon white peppercorns, toasted

1 tablespoon fennel seeds, toasted

1 head of garlic, sliced in half across the cloves

2 banana shallots, sliced in half

2 litres vegetable oil

4 garlic cloves, pounded to a paste

1 large egg, beaten

150g cold cooked jasmine rice

20ml soy sauce

4 tablespoons burnt chilli dipping sauce (see page 146), to serve

10g chives, chopped, to garnish

This is the brunch of champions. There is nothing more satisfying to a hungry chef than a big bowl of egg fried rice and crispy pork belly with a smoky, spicy and sour burnt chilli dipping sauce poured all over. If I ever open a kitchen that served breakfast, I would serve just this and I would be a millionaire (unless the whole planet turned vegan, of course).

First, blanch the pork belly to remove all the impurities. In a large saucepan, heat enough water to submerge the pork belly in, and when simmering, add the pork belly and 2 tablespoons of the salt. Simmer for 10–12 minutes until the pork is warm throughout, regularly skimming off the scum that forms on the surface of the water. When cooked, rinse the pork belly under cold running water.

Meanwhile, bring a separate large saucepan of water to a simmer. To this, add all the spices, the garlic, shallots, the remaining salt and the warm pork belly, making sure that it is completely submerged in the water. Cover with a lid and simmer on a low heat for 3 hours. The pork will soften slowly and take on the flavour of all the spices. When cooked, remove the pork belly from the pan and set it aside. Strain and reserve the liquor.

Heat the oil in a large, deep saucepan to 160°C. Carefully place the pork belly in the pan, making sure that it is submerged in the oil. Deep-fry for 8–10 minutes until the belly is crispy, but be careful of spitting fat. Remove the belly from the oil and set aside to cool slightly, then slice along the belly widthways to get half crispy, half soft thick chunks of pork belly bacon.

Meanwhile, heat 2 tablespoons of oil in a large wok to a high temperature. Fry the garlic until it starts to turn golden brown, then add the beaten egg and stir a few times so that it scrambles in big chunks. Don't stir too much; just enough to stop it from sticking. Add the rice and scrape constantly, making sure it doesn't stick to the wok (lower the heat a little if the rice sticks too much). Stir-fry the rice for a further 3–4 minutes until it begins to darken a little and smells a little smoky. Add the soy sauce and about 30ml liquor from braising the pork belly – just enough to loosen the rice. Serve the rice in bowls, topped with the pork belly, the chilli dipping sauce and a sprinkling of chives.

STIR-FRIED MUSHROOMS, SOY, CASHEWS AND FLOWERING CHIVES

4 garlic cloves, peeled

10g ginger, peeled and roughly chopped

1 tablespoon roughly chopped coriander roots

a pinch of coarse sea salt

2 tablespoons vegetable oil

4 field mushrooms, peeled and stems removed, cut into quarters

8 shiitake mushrooms, roughly sliced

2 king oyster mushrooms, sliced lengthways into thick chunks

50g pak choi, cut into bite-sized pieces

2g enoki mushrooms

2 tablespoons toasted cashew nuts

3 long red chillies, sliced into rounds and soaked in a little cold water to remove some seeds

1 tablespoon light soy sauce

80ml vegetable stock

1 teaspoon caster sugar

80ml coconut cream

10g Thai sweet basil, torn

8 Thai shallots, peeled and roughly sliced

steamed jasmine rice, to serve (optional)

This is a simple stir-fry and the fact of the matter is, it's tasty with any variety of mushrooms, so have a play around. At Farang, we like to include fresh mustard greens and sometimes even fennel, so by no means is this a recipe set in stone, think of it as a guideline and have some fun with it.

Pound the garlic, ginger and coriander roots to a paste in a pestle and mortar or food processor, using the salt as an abrasive to help combine the ingredients.

Heat the oil in a large wok over a high temperature, then add the field, shiitake and oyster mushrooms, tossing frequently but allowing them to colour from the heat of the wok. You'll notice the mushrooms will start to smoke as they cook in the oil – mushrooms have an amazing way of soaking up all that smokiness, so keep going for about 2 minutes until the mushrooms are soft and begin to take on a light brown colour.

Next, add the paste to the wok along with the pak choi, enoki mushrooms, cashew nuts and chillies, and stir-fry for another minute until the paste begins to turn golden brown. Deglaze the wok with the soy sauce, stock, sugar and coconut cream, then simmer until the vegetables have softened.

Throw in the basil and the Thai shallots and give everything a good mix. The stir-fry should be savoury, creamy, fresh and a little spicy with an umami twist from the mushrooms. Serve immediately either on its own or with steamed jasmine rice.

ROASTED THAI GARLIC AND DRIED SHRIMP STIR-FRIED MORNING GLORY

SERVES 2
AS A SIDE

VE
OPTIONAL

20g Thai garlic, peeled and bruised (or 6 garlic cloves)

3 mixed red and green bird's-eye chillies

I teaspoon coarse sea salt

I tablespoon vegetable oil

10g dried shrimp, ground to a floss (optional)

100g *ong choi* (morning glory), roughly chopped

50ml vegetable stock

½ teaspoon caster sugar

I tablespoon light soy sauce

Morning glory is a type of water spinach, known as *ong choi* in Thailand, and it is typically stir-fried with a little stock and seasoning and served as a side or with rice. I have seen Thai street vendors make the dish in a wok and then, using both hands, toss the stir-fry behind them over the top of their heads. A partner will then be stood over the road who catches the stir-fry on a plate and then serves to customers straight away. I wouldn't recommend this service style myself, but why not, right? *Ong choi* can be difficult to get, so if you cannot find it use spinach, *choi sum* or cabbage.

Pound the garlic and chillies to a paste in a pestle and mortar, using the salt as an abrasive to help combine the ingredients. Meanwhile, heat the oil in a wok on a high heat, then add the paste and dried shrimp (if using), scraping and tossing until the paste begins to turn golden brown. Add the morning glory and stir-fry for a further minute until the stalks begin to turn translucent and soft. Be sure though not to cook for too long as the morning glory will lose its vibrant green fresh colour.

Deglaze the wok with the stock, sugar and soy sauce, and toss a few times to mix well. Check the seasoning: it should be light, fishy and salty. Serve immediately.

STIR FRIES AND LITTLE THINGS

75

STIR-FRIED BEEF WITH ROASTED CHILLI JAM, SHALLOTS AND KALE

200g flat-iron steak, sliced against the grain into 2cm thick pieces

1 teaspoon cumin, toasted and ground to a powder

1 teaspoon coriander seeds, toasted and ground to a powder

½ teaspoon chilli powder

3 tablespoons vegetable oil

20g crispy chilli and coconut jam (see page 161)

4 banana shallots, peeled and thickly sliced lengthways

30g kale, stems removed, torn into bite-sized pieces and blanched in boiling salted water for 2 minutes, then refreshed in cold water

50ml beef stock

1 tablespoon fish sauce

1 tablespoon palm sugar

1 teaspoon distilled white vinegar

2 tablespoons thick tamarind water

steamed jasmine rice, to serve (optional)

This is another great stir-fry, tasty either alongside other dishes, or on its own with some steamed jasmine rice. Any fast-cook cut of beef can be used, as by stir-frying in smoking hot oil it is possible to char the meat on all sides and still keep it rare in the middle, which adds a smokiness to the dish only found from cooking in the wok. I like to use flat iron steak as its marbled fat allows it to stir-fry juicy and tender.

Place the steak in a bowl and add the cumin, coriander seeds, chilli powder and 1 tablespoon of the oil, then mix together with your hands. Set aside within arm's reach of the wok alongside all the other ingredients, ready to make the stir-fry.

Heat the remaining oil in a large wok over a high heat until it is smoking hot. Add the beef and give the wok a little shake to make sure the meat doesn't stick to it (the coating of oil on the meat and in the wok should stop it from sticking completely). Stir-fry the beef for about 30 seconds until it is sealed on all sides. Add the chilli jam, shallots and the blanched kale and stir-fry for another minute or so until the vegetables have softened.

Deglaze the wok with the stock, fish sauce, palm sugar, vinegar and tamarind water, tossing the ingredients once more to combine fully. The dish should taste rich, sweet, salty, smoky and sour, and goes perfectly with a bowl of steamed jasmine rice.

600ml fish stock

3 tablespoons light soy sauce

1 teaspoon chilli powder

1 teaspoon caster sugar

½ teaspoon sea salt

¼ cucumber, peeled and sliced into thin rounds

1 teaspoon dried shrimp

1 large egg, beaten

10g Thai sweet basil (or Italian basil), torn

¼ teaspoon ground white pepper

3–4 tablespoons cooked jasmine rice (optional)

DRIED SHRIMP, EGG
AND CUCUMBER SOUP

This has been a staple quick food fix for me for a long time. It always does the job, whether I'm hung over, feeling ill or just bloody hungry. It's not a bad breakfast either. Try it with 3–4 tablespoons of cooked jasmine rice put into it for an extra fill – lovely.

Add the stock, soy sauce, chilli powder, sugar, salt and cucumber to a saucepan and slowly bring to a simmer, then cook for a few minutes to soften the cucumber. Add the dried shrimp and continue to cook until the shrimp and cucumber both are softened. Swirl the liquid and pour the egg in so that it scrambles as it comes into contact with the hot soup. Throw in the basil, white pepper and jasmine rice, if using, and serve immediately. Adjust the seasoning if necessary to suit your own taste.

SEUA-RONG-HAI GRILLED BEEF

By Narisa Chauvidul-Aw
Founder of ThaiSmile Group ~ thaismile.com

SERVES 4–5
AS A STARTER OR SNACK

3 tablespoons uncooked glutinuous rice

3 kaffir lime leaves, torn slightly

400g sirloin steak

I tablespoon honey

2 tablespoons light soy sauce

¼ cup fresh green peppercorns, lightly crushed

FOR THE TAMARIND DIP

3 tablespoons tamarind juice

I tablespoon granulated sugar

I tablespoon lime juice

3 tablespoons fish sauce

I tablespoon dried chilli powder

I tablespoon ground toasted rice (see above)

This is one of my favourite dishes from the North East of Thailand, where it is known as 'Weeping Tiger'. There are various stories to back up the name, but my guess is that the chillies in the dipping sauce are so hot they can make a tiger weep.

First make the toasted rice by placing the rice in a dry frying pan together with the kaffir lime leaves. Dry fry for 10–15 minutes on a medium heat until the rice turns golden brown. Using either a food blender or a pestle and mortar, ground the toasted rice until it is as fine a powder as possible so it adds crunch, flavour and texture to each mouthful and does not hurt the teeth. If it is not ground finely enough it can sometimes not be nice in a salad.

Stab the steak all over with a fork, then place it in a shallow dish, add the honey and light soy sauce and leave to marinate for at least I hour.

Preheat the oven to 200°C/gas mark 6. Place the steak on a baking tray, press the crushed peppercorns on top and cook for 10 minutes for medium-rare or 15 minutes for medium. Remove from the oven, cover with foil and leave to rest.

Make the dipping sauce by stirring together the tamarind juice, sugar, lime juice and fish sauce until the sugar has dissolved, then add the chilli powder and toasted rice. It should taste sour, sweet and salty.

To serve, slice the beef against the grain and arrange on a plate. Scatter the ground rice over the top and serve the tamarind dipping sauce in a small dipping bowl on the side so that the beef can be dipped into it with ease.

STIR FRIES AND LITTLE THINGS

CHILLI JAM CLAMS
WITH SWEET BASIL

SERVES 2

10g ginger, peeled and
roughly chopped

4 garlic cloves, peeled

2 red bird's-eye chillies

a pinch of coarse sea salt

1 tablespoon vegetable oil

1 tablespoon palm sugar
(or soft dark brown sugar)

300ml hot vegetable stock

50g crispy chilli and coconut
jam (see page 161)

400g clams, purged in
water with 1 teaspoon
bicarbonate of soda for
4 hours, but ideally overnight

25g Thai sweet basil
(or Italian basil), torn,
plus extra to serve

2 long red chillies,
roughly sliced

1 tablespoon fish sauce

200ml coconut cream

2 kaffir lime leaves,
finely sliced (optional)

1 lime, cut into wedges,
to serve

**Always remember to purge your clams before sticking
them in your stir-fry, otherwise you will end up having
a sandy surprise at the bottom of your dinner bowl!
The most effective technique I know is to submerge them
in cold water with a little bicarbonate of soda stirred in.
Leave for at least a few hours, preferably overnight, in the
fridge. They should release all the sand and dirt that would
otherwise remain within the shell.**

Pound the ginger, garlic and bird's-eye chillies to a paste in a pestle and
mortar, using the salt as an abrasive to help combine the ingredients.

Heat the oil in a wok, then add the paste and fry for a few minutes,
stirring it constantly to prevent it sticking. When the paste begins to crisp,
add the palm sugar and fry for a further minute to caramelise; the paste
will darken slightly.

Pour in the stock and chilli and coconut jam, bring to a simmer,
then add the clams. Simmer for about 3 minutes until the clams have
opened (discard any that remain closed). Add the basil, red chillies, fish
sauce and coconut cream, and carefully stir together. Sprinkle the kaffir
lime leaves over the top.

Serve the clams in bowls topped with a wedge of lime and more basil.
Have finger bowls and lots of napkins on the table!

200ml fish stock

2 tablespoons fish sauce

½ teaspoon coarse sea salt

10g galangal, peeled, chopped into 2cm pieces and bruised

2 coriander roots (5g), roughly bruised

2 green bird's-eye chillies, bruised

2 sticks lemongrass, cut into 2cm pieces and bruised

3 kaffir lime leaves (2 slightly torn, 1 fine julienned, to serve)

8 Thai shallots, peeled and slightly bruised

500g clams, purged in water with 1 teaspoon bicarbonate of soda for 4 hours, but ideally overnight

juice of 1 lime

1 tablespoon tamarind paste

100ml vegetable oil

1 head of garlic, sliced in half across the cloves

5g dried shrimp

a pinch of coarse sea salt

1 teaspoon palm sugar

1 teaspoon chilli powder

CLAMS IN TOM YUM BROTH WITH SHRIMP OIL AND ROASTED GARLIC

Popular not just in Thailand but also in neighbouring countries such as Cambodia, Malaysia and Singapore, *tom yum* has certainly built itself a delicious reputation. It's eaten with a range of different proteins and vegetables but my favourite is seafood. Here the clams are the star of the show, with a flavoursome, *tom yum* broth steamed into them.

In a medium saucepan, place the fish stock, fish sauce, salt, galangal, coriander roots, chillies, lemongrass, torn kaffir lime leaves and Thai shallots and simmer until the vegetables have softened.

Add the clams and gently stir to ensure that all the clams are covered in the broth. Cover with a lid and steam for 3–4 minutes until the clams have opened (discard any that remain closed), then add the lime juice and tamarind paste.

Meanwhile, preheat the oven to 180°C/gas mark 4. Pour the oil into a small tray and place the garlic, cut-side down, into the oil. Roast for 20–25 minutes until the flesh has softened and is slightly translucent. Remove the tray from the oven and stir in the dried shrimp so that it slowly roasts in the heat of the garlic oil. Once cool, use a fork to pick out the garlic flesh. Pound the roasted garlic, garlic oil, a pinch of salt, the palm sugar and chilli powder in a pestle and mortar or food processor. It should taste roasted, fishy, spicy and salty.

Serve the clams in bowls with a spoonful of the roasted garlic oil and a sprinkling of julienned lime leaves. Have finger bowls at the ready.

SWEET FISH SAUCE WITH SESAME TEMPURA CHICKEN BREAST

SERVES 4

VE
OPTIONAL

200g tempura flour

I teaspoon table salt

230g rice flour

50g tapioca flour

550ml ice-cold sparkling water

2 litres sunflower oil

4 chicken breasts
(about 400g), sliced
widthways into 1cm strips

½ teaspoon sea salt

100ml hot chicken stock

300ml fish sauce

200g caster sugar

2 spring onions, thinly sliced

4 long red chillies,
thinly sliced

10g mint leaves, shredded

10g coriander leaves,
finely chopped

I teaspoon sesame seeds

I lime, cut into wedges,
to serve

These are perfect for sharing, either as a starter or snack, but so good you'll probably not want to share them with anyone. Sweet, salty, crispy and spicy pieces of tempura chicken breast that put your local fried chicken joint to absolute shame. I've sweetened the fish sauce with sugar, but it can be sweetened quite deliciously by leaving a few pieces of fresh pineapple in the bottle to infuse. The fructose gives for a more rounded, less 'in your face' fish sauce flavour.

Start by making the batter. In a bowl, sift the tempura flour, table salt, 100g of the rice flour and the tapioca flour together. Slowly add 500ml of the sparkling water, stirring the batter with a fork (this will leave a few small lumps in the batter which add extra texture once fried; using a whisk would make a completely smooth batter). The batter should be thick enough to cling to your fingers but loose enough run off in one motion without dripping. Add a little more sparkling water if needed. Place the batter in the freezer while you prepare the remaining ingredients (however, unless you want a batter ice lolly it's best not to get too far ahead!).

Heat the oil in a large, wide saucepan to about 220°C. Sift another 100g rice flour onto a tray and add the chicken strips, making sure all the chicken is thoroughly coated.

Check the temperature of the oil by dropping a little cold batter into it – if it bubbles and turns light golden brown after 30 seconds, you're good to go. Using chopsticks or tongs, individually dip the chicken strips into the batter, then carefully drop them into the hot oil, cooking 5 or 6 strips at a time to ensure they cook evenly and that the temperature of the oil doesn't drop too much. Cook for about 3 minutes, then transfer onto kitchen paper to drain and sprinkle with the sea salt. Keep warm in a medium oven while the remaining chicken is being cooked.

Meanwhile, make a thick, pourable paste by sifting the remaining 30g rice flour into the stock and whisking energetically until there are no lumps.

Heat the fish sauce and sugar together in a large saucepan and whisk in the thickened chicken stock, making sure that there are no lumps. Simmer for 15–20 minutes, stirring regularly, until the flour has cooked out and the sugar has caramelised and turned silky and shiny. Check for seasoning: the glaze should taste sweet, salty and savoury, so adjust it if you need to.

Check that the chicken is piping hot before serving. Coat it in the glaze, then top with the spring onions, chillies, mint, coriander and sesame seeds. Serve with wedges of lime.

STIR FRIES AND LITTLE THINGS

83

150–200ml vegetable oil

2 large eggs

50g red curry paste
(see page 163)

250g beef mince

4 banana shallots,
sliced lengthways into
1cm thick pieces

1 teaspoon caster sugar

2 tablespoons fish sauce

1 tablespoon thick
tamarind water

10g coriander leaves,
chopped

10g Thai sweet basil
(or Italian basil)

10g mint leaves, torn in half

10g *pak chi farang*
(Thai flat-leaf coriander)

210g watercress, roughly
chopped

1 lime, cut into wedges

steamed jasmine rice,
to serve

MINCED RED CURRY BEEF
WITH LIME, FRESH HERBS AND WOK-FRIED EGG

This is my version of an almost dry beef red curry; the beef is cooked hard on a hot heat with red curry paste and herbs, creating a delicious spicy salad. Serve accompanied with raw cabbage, sliced cucumber and jasmine rice to make a filling meal out of it. A runny egg over the top that the diner can break into themselves is a must.

The best way to set yourself up for cooking this dish is to separate all the prepared ingredients into bowls and place them within arm's length of the cooker for easy access while cooking. The eggs will be cooked first, so crack them into two separate bowls for convenience and have a plate lined with kitchen paper handy to put them on.

Heat the oil in a large wok to a high heat. When it is sizzling hot, carefully pour in one of the eggs; be careful of splattering oil as it hits the wok. As soon as the egg touches the oil it will begin to cook very fast. Leave it for about 10 seconds, then gently unstick it from the base of the wok, being careful not to split the egg yolk. When the egg white is cooked and the yolk still looks runny (about 20–30 seconds), remove the egg using a slotted wok spoon and place it on the draining plate. Repeat with the second egg.

In the same oil, add the red curry paste and stir constantly to ensure it doesn't stick to the wok. When the paste begins to darken, add the beef mince and continue frying on a high heat, scraping and stirring to ensure it doesn't stick to the wok. When the beef is hot throughout, add the banana shallots, sugar, fish sauce, tamarind water and herbs, then toss all together. The heat from the wok should quickly soften the banana shallots while leaving a textural crunch.

Serve the red curry beef in bowls with some steamed jasmine rice and the fried egg and lime on top.

1 small (800g) chicken

1 pomelo (or pink grapefruit)

4 small cucumbers, sliced on the bias

10 small red shallots, thickly sliced

2 spring onions, roughly chopped

25g roughly chopped mint

25g roughly chopped coriander, leaves and stalks

FOR THE DRESSING

3 long red chillies, deseeded and roughly chopped

2 small green scuds (bird's eye chillies)

a pinch of coarse sea salt

4 small garlic cloves, peeled

2 tablespoons caster sugar

120ml fish sauce

juice of 2 limes

a pinch of chilli powder

a pinch of deep-fried garlic

SILKEN CHICKEN POMELO AND HERB SALAD

By Annita Potter (Mim)
Executive Chef, Long Chim

Pomelo is the largest citrus fruit on the planet and comes in many varieties and flavours. Most commonly the flesh is white and sweet, they can also be found blood red and bitter or sour in flavour. For this dish white, sweeter pomelo's are ideal, their flavour works well with the sour, salty and spicy notes through the dressing. When choosing a pomelo pick the heaviest one – the heavier the fruit the more juice within, and more flavoursome.

Bring a large pot of salted water to the boil, add the chicken and cover with a lid, simmer for 20 minutes, then remove from the heat and leave for 15 minutes.

Remove the chicken and place in a bowl of iced water for a further 20 minutes. Strain the cooking liquid into a jug and set aside. When the chicken has cooled, remove the flesh, discarding the skin and bones, shred and set aside.

Peel the pomelo, divide it into segments, and combine with the cucumber, shallots, spring onions, mint and coriander.

To make the dressing, put the red chillies in a large pestle and mortar, along with the small scuds, a good pinch of salt and the garlic cloves, and pound until you have a fine paste. Add the sugar and dissolve slightly, then add the fish sauce, lime juice, a pinch of chilli powder and the deep-fried garlic. Taste for seasoning. It should be hot, salty and sour.

Place the salad ingredients in a bowl, pour over most of your dressing and taste for its overall seasoning. It may need an extra tablespoon of fish sauce and squeeze of lime to finish.

3 BARBECUE

4 large quails, spatchcocked

I stick lemongrass, thin end sliced many times so it can be used as a glazing brush

10g Thai shallots, sliced, to garnish

3 spring onions, sliced, to garnish

10g mint, roughly torn, to garnish

10g coriander, roughly torn, to garnish

sticky rice, to serve

FOR THE PASTE

I tablespoon chopped coriander roots

10g ginger, peeled and roughly chopped

6 red bird's-eye chillies, stems removed and chopped

8 garlic cloves, peeled

½ teaspoon coarse sea salt

100ml kecap manis (or any sweet soy sauce)

50ml maltose

10ml thick tamarind water

I tablespoon sesame oil

25ml whisky

50ml fish sauce

WHISKY AND MALTOSE BARBECUE QUAILS

Quails, because of their small size, are perfect for cooking on the bone over the high heat of a barbecue, where their natural sweetness is complemented by the smokiness of the wood. I see no benefit in taking the time to remove the bones, when retaining them keeps the meat so moist. I like to eat them accompanied with some sticky glutinous rice and a fiery *som tam* salad (see page 92).

Start by making the paste. Pound the coriander roots, ginger, chillies and garlic to a coarse paste in a pestle and mortar or food processor, using the salt as an abrasive. Add all the other paste ingredients and mix well. Place the quails into this sauce and marinate for a minimum of I hour and a maximum of 6 hours; if you leave them any longer they will begin to cure from the salt content and, although this is delicious, it's not what we're after for this dish.

Place the marinated quails skin-side up over hot embers; this allows the skin to dry slightly as the other side cooks and helps crisp the skin when it is later put in direct contact with the heat. Cook the quails for 5–6 minutes on each side, making sure to keep basting the meat with the marinade using the lemongrass brush. They are ready when the outside is crisp, charred and caramelised and the inside is piping hot. Make a small incision with the tip of a sharp knife all the way to the bone – if the meat is still a little pink around the bones, cook for a few more minutes. For best results, use a temperature probe and take the quails off the barbecue when the core temperature reaches 66–68°C, then rest for 5 minutes before serving.

Meanwhile, bring the leftover marinade to the boil and simmer for 5 minutes until all the sugars have caramelised and the sauce has thickened slightly. Taste for seasoning: it should be sweet and salty, so adjust if necessary.

Serve the quails stacked on a plate with the warm sauce drizzled over the top. Scatter with the Thai shallots, spring onions, mint and coriander. Serve with sticky rice, finger bowls and lots of napkins.

TIPS

Spatchcocking the quail means they can be easily cooked on the barbecue. Either ask your butcher to do it or do it yourself using a pair of scissors.

GRILLED LANGOUSTINES, GREEN MANGO AND RED NAM YUM

8 langoustines (300–400g total weight)

3 tablespoons softened butter

I teaspoon coarse sea salt

FOR THE RED NAM YUM

2 tablespoons chopped coriander roots

8 garlic cloves, peeled

6 long red chillies, stems removed, seeds scraped out and roughly chopped

2 tablespoons caster sugar

juice of 5 limes

juice of 2 mandarins (or clementines)

4 tablespoons fish sauce

10g mint leaves, roughly torn

10g coriander leaves, roughly torn

I green mango, peeled and grated or julienned

Langoustines aren't on enough restaurant menus in my opinion. They belong to the lobster family, are similar in appearance to crayfish but, unlike crayfish, live in salt water. Smaller langoustines have a sweet meat that is relatively simple to get to with your fingers once cooked, if you don't mind getting a little messy. They don't survive very long out of the water, and most are frozen on the boat, which makes them hard to get fresh, so be sure to buy only what you are going to cook that day. If you can't get green mango, any crunchy sour fruit will work well.

Light the barbecue to a high heat and, while it is heating up, prepare the langoustines. I like cooking these over wood as they take on the smoky flavour so well, which works in harmony with their natural sweetness. Place one langoustine flat-side down on a chopping board. Hold the thorax between your thumb and index finger, place the tip of a sharp knife along the lateral line that runs down the thorax, and lower the blade through the langoustine. Cut it in half down the centre so you end up with two exact halves. Remove the sand sack, which is located near the head – it should come out in one piece – and using tweezers, remove the vein from whichever side it ends up in. Repeat this process with all the langoustines.

Rub the inside of the langoustines with the butter and a pinch of salt, then grill for 2–3 minutes on each side until the flesh has firmed up and is hot throughout. It's nice to get a little char on the shells too for presentation.

Meanwhile, pound the coriander roots, garlic, then chillies (in that order) to a coarse paste in a pestle and mortar, using a pinch of salt as an abrasive, if necessary. Add the sugar and pound for a few more seconds. This should give you a relatively smooth paste, though a little chunk is not the end of the world. Finally, add the lime and mandarin juices and the fish sauce. The sauce should taste sweet, salty, sour and hot. Exact quantities are impossible to give, as the strength of the ingredients varies depending on where they are grown, so adjust the seasoning to suit your tastes.

Gently toss the langoustines in the red *nam yum* dressing, along with the mint, coriander and green mango, and serve with finger bowls and an empty bowl to dispose of the langoustine shells.

SERVES 2-3

GRILLED TIGER PRAWNS
AND MANDARIN
SOM TAM SALAD

8–10 prawns, cleaned, deveined and outer shells removed

1 teaspoon fish sauce

1 teaspoon vegetable oil

FOR THE SOM TAM SALAD

4 garlic cloves, peeled

2 teaspoons dried shrimp

a pinch of sea salt

1 tablespoon peanuts, fried

3 red bird's-eye chillies

10g green beans

30g cherry tomatoes

200g shredded papaya

10–15g palm sugar (or soft dark brown sugar)

20ml thick tamarind water

juice of 2 limes

½ lime, chopped

juice of 1 mandarin

Som tam **has fast become one of the most widely eaten and popular salads to come out of Asia. It originates from Lao, but now has many well-known variations from all over. This version is one I created for Farang. The use of mandarin, which adds a sweetness, along with the juices of the grilled prawns, makes it a stand out dish. Try it with the grilled quail on page 90 and some sticky glutinous rice for a proper feed.**

Coat the prawns in the fish sauce and oil, then place them on a hot grill for 3–4 minutes until the side in contact with the heat has turned pink. Turn the prawns over and repeat on the other side until they are hot throughout. Remove from the heat and set aside.

Pound the garlic and dried shrimp in a large pestle and mortar, using the salt as an abrasive. Then pound in the peanuts to break them up just enough to mix through the salad; be careful not to over-pound them or they will turn into peanut butter.

Next, one by one, add the chillies, green beans, tomatoes, half the grilled prawns and papaya to the mortar, bruising them as you go to distribute the flavours.

Add the palm sugar, tamarind water, lime juice, chopped lime and the juice of 1 mandarin. Give the salad a final bruising to ensure that all ingredients are packed full of the flavoursome dressing, making sure that the palm sugar has completely dissolved in the dressing, otherwise someone will get an unexpected sweet mouthful. Taste the dressing to check that it suits your tastes – it should be sweet, salty, sour and spicy with a hint of bitterness from the lime zest. Adjust the seasoning if necessary, then serve the salad with the remaining prawns arranged on top.

20g coconut (or vegetable) oil

200g green curry paste
(see page 167)

3g kaffir lime leaves, torn

15ml fish sauce

10–15g palm sugar (or soft
brown sugar)

300ml hot chicken stock

300ml coconut cream

6 free-range chicken thighs
on the bone (500–600g total
weight)

100g new potatoes, halved

80g baby sweetcorn, sliced at
an angle

80g green beans, sliced in
half lengthways

10g wild ginger (krachai),
peeled and julienned
(or regular ginger)

10g Thai sweet basil
(or Italian basil), torn

steamed jasmine rice,
to serve

a piece of wood for smoking
on the BBQ (my favourite is
hickory)

SMOKED CHICKEN
GREEN CURRY

When cooking chicken over a fierce heat such as a barbecue, it's always best to marinate or brine it first. Now, you can honestly spend a lifetime researching the brining process and some people do, however we don't have time for that! Suffice to say that by leaving raw meat in contact with salt and/or sugar and moisture before cooking, you allow it to take on flavour. This recipe uses the green curry paste to marinate the chicken, meaning it's packed full of goodness by the time it hits the barbecue.

Heat the coconut oil in a large saucepan over a high heat, then add the green curry paste and kaffir lime leaves and stir regularly until the paste begins to split like scrambled eggs – this will take 6–8 minutes. You will notice that the smell of the ingredients changes from raw to fragrant. At this point, add 10ml fish sauce and allow it to cook into the paste for 1 minute (don't add too much as it is strong and you can always add, but never take away). Next, add the sugar and cook for a minute or so until melted and beginning to caramelise – this is noticeable as the paste begins to darken.

Now it's time to loosen the curry with liquids. Add half the chicken stock and 100ml of the coconut cream to the pan, then remove from the heat and allow to cool. When cool, use a little of the curry to marinate the chicken thighs; use enough to coat them, then refrigerate the chicken to allow the flavours to infuse for a minimum of 2 hours, but ideally overnight.

Light the barbecue and wait for the coals to glow red. Place the piece of wood onto the coals and wait for it to catch fire and begin to smoke. At this point, add the chicken thighs skin-side up, lower the barbecue lid so that the meat is engulfed by the smoke and cook for 3–4 minutes on one side. Turn the chicken pieces over and repeat the process until the skin is crispy and golden brown and the chicken is piping hot.

Next, return the remaining green curry to the pan and bring back to a simmer. Add any excess from the marinated chicken, then add the remaining stock. Add the potatoes and cook for about 8 minutes until they begin to soften. Add the sweetcorn and green beans and cook for a further 5 minutes until all the vegetables are softened but still retain a little bite. Add the hot chicken thighs, the remaining coconut cream and the wild ginger and basil. Check you are happy with the seasoning, add the rest of the fish sauce if needed, and serve immediately. This dish is best served with steamed jasmine rice.

SERVES 2

2 tablespoons vegetable
(or groundnut) oil

50g choi sum, chopped into
3cm pieces

20g green beans, topped and
tailed and cut into thirds

6 asparagus spears, tough
ends removed, sliced in half
lengthways

2 green bird's-eye chillies

4 garlic cloves, peeled

1 teaspoon wild ginger
(*krachai*), peeled and roughly
chopped (or regular ginger)

½ teaspoon coarse sea salt

100ml hot vegetable stock

1 tablespoon light soy sauce
(or fish sauce)

¼ teaspoon white
peppercorns, toasted and
ground to a powder

1 teaspoon caster sugar

crispy garlic (see page 161),
to garnish (optional)

crispy shallots (see page 161),
to garnish (optional)

steamed jasmine rice,
to serve (optional)

GRILLED GREENS, CHOI SUM, BEANS, ASPARAGUS, SOY AND WHITE PEPPER

Charring the vegetables over the barbecue before cooking adds an unexpected depth of flavour to the broth. I've served it as a side at numerous pop-ups and did not realise how good it was until I got the customer feedback; many people say it's their favourite dish. Not always the best thing to hear when you know it takes so little time compared to most other dishes! You can use any variety of vegetables, so don't limit yourselves to just these. I love it with cabbage or kale, even cucumber.

Light the barbecue. If you have the option, use wood as you want as much smoky flavour as possible to infuse the vegetables. Use 1 tablespoon of the oil to lightly coat all the vegetables and when the embers are glowing red, place them over the heat and turn often until all sides are lightly charred – there is no need to cook the vegetables through as this process is simply for imparting the smoky flavour.

Next, in a pestle and mortar, pound the chillies, garlic and wild ginger to make a coarse paste, using the sea salt as an abrasive.

Heat the remaining oil in a large wok, then add the paste and fry until it begins to turn golden brown, stirring constantly to ensure even cooking. Add the charred vegetables to the wok and toss for about 1 minute on a high heat to ensure that everything is cooked through and softened, but try to leave a little bite. Add the stock, soy sauce, peppercorns and sugar and toss through the stir-fry; it should all fuse together to create a delicious, light, smoky broth.

Serve the stir-fry immediately. For added texture, garnish with crispy garlic and shallots left over from making the crispy chilli and coconut jam on page 161. This is great served as a side or with steamed jasmine rice as a main.

1 tablespoon jasmine rice

500ml vegetable oil

10g fresh curry leaves
(optional)

½ teaspoon table salt

2 beef steaks (roughly
150g each)

100ml kecap manis (or any
kind of sweet soy sauce)

4 tablespoons *nam jim jaew*
(see page 151)

10g coriander, chopped

GRILLED BEEF AND SMOKY NAM JIM JAEW WITH ROASTED RICE AND SALTED CURRY LEAVES

This dish lets the grill do all the talking. There is something particularly satisfying about placing vegetables over an open fire and leaving them to turn into a delicious, smoky sauce. And it's an unbeatable combination when eaten with beef cooked in this way. Use whatever cut is your favourite; I like bavette for its depth of flavour.

Preheat the oven to 180°C/gas mark 4. Place the rice on a baking tray and bake for 35–40 minutes until golden brown. Allow to cool, then grind to a fine powder in a pestle and mortar. Be sure to grind the rice as finely as possible or it will not be pleasant to eat; the idea is for the rice to add texture to an otherwise soft dish.

Meanwhile, heat the oil to 180°C in a small saucepan. Check the temperature of the oil by placing a curry leaf into it – it should bubble gently and take around 15–20 seconds to crisp without losing its green colour. If it goes brown straight away the oil is too hot so you will need to let it cool slightly. Fry all the curry leaves, then drain onto kitchen paper. Sprinkle the leaves with the salt while they are still warm so that the salt sticks to them a little.

To prepare the steaks, place them onto a plate and rub all over with the kecap manis. Allow to rest for 20 minutes so that the meat comes to room temperature, then place the steaks over red-hot embers and cook evenly on both sides to your liking. The sugar in the kecap manis caramelises around the meat, giving it an extraordinary colour and flavour. Once the steak is cooked, allow it to rest for 5 minutes before serving.

To serve, slice the meat against the grain and arrange it onto a plate. Put the *nam jim jaew* onto the plate and scatter the ground rice, coriander and curry leaves over the meat.

SARDINES with SMOKY TOMATO and PORK RELISH with HERBS and VEGETABLES

SERVES 4

GF

4 medium sardines (150–200g each), cleaned and gutted

I teaspoon coarse sea salt

10g bunch of coriander

10g bunch of Thai sweet basil (or Italian basil)

10g bunch of dill

½ cucumber, sliced into rounds

I baby gem lettuce, leaves separated

I chicory, core removed

FOR THE NAM PRIK ONG RELISH

400g minced pork belly (20% fat)

50g fresh cherry tomatoes, halved

2 tablespoons chopped coriander roots

20g ginger, peeled and roughly chopped

20g garlic, peeled

I teaspoon ground white pepper

100g rendered pork fat

300g red curry paste

50g tua noa (dried fermented soya beans), toasted and ground to a fine powder

I tablespoon thick tamarind water

2 tablespoons palm sugar (or soft dark brown sugar)

I tablespoon fish sauce

I teaspoon smoked chilli powder, to garnish

10g Thai shallots, peeled and sliced, to garnish

2 spring onions, thinly sliced, to garnish

This relish is known as *nam prik ong* in Thailand and originates from the Northern regions. In the kitchen, we always refer to it as 'Thai Bolognese', as its rich tomato and beef flavour has similarities in taste and appearance. Traditionally eaten with omelette and pork scratchings, it also goes really well with oily fish such as sardines or mackerel and is a delicious dip for raw vegetables.

Start by making the *nam prik ong* relish. In a large bowl, and using both hands, mix the pork mince and tomatoes together, making sure to be thorough as the acid in the tomatoes helps to break down the fat and aids the cooking process. Leave at room temperature for 30 minutes while you prepare the rest.

Pound the coriander roots, ginger, garlic and pepper to a paste in a pestle and mortar or food processor. In a large non-stick frying pan, heat the rendered pork fat (set aside a little to cook the sardines) on a high heat, then add the paste and continue to fry until the paste starts to turn golden brown, then add the red curry paste and the *tua noa* and fry for a further 15 minutes on a high heat, scraping the bottom of the pan regularly to ensure that the mixture does not stick to it. Once the paste begins to darken, add the mince and tomatoes and fry for a further 25–30 minutes, turning the heat down to medium once the pork is cooked through. Be sure to keep stirring and scraping the relish regularly to ensure that it does not stick. After the mix has become one and the fat begins to split and floats, add the tamarind water, sugar and fish sauce and cook for a further minute or so until the sugar has caramelised. Remove from the heat. This is now ready to serve and should be served hot. Any leftovers can be stored in an airtight container in the fridge for 3–4 days.

Meanwhile, light the barbecue to a high heat. Coat the sardines in a thin layer of pork fat, then sprinkle them with the salt. Place the fish on the grills directly over red hot embers and grill for 3–4 minutes on either side until the skin is golden brown and crispy and the flesh is cooked all the way through. For best results, use a temperature probe and take the fish off the barbecue when it reaches 65–68°C, then leave to rest for 3 minutes before serving. The fish should be about 70°C after resting as it continues to cook.

Serve the *nam prik ong* in a bowl and top with the smoked chilli powder, Thai shallots and spring onions. Arrange the herbs, vegetables and sardines around the bowl so people can use their hands to pick up what they want and dip into the relish. It's a fun sharing dish if you eat it this way. Alternatively, you can serve individual portions – it's up to you.

GRILLED MACKEREL WITH A PICKLED BEAN SPROUT SALAD, ROASTED CHILLI OIL, PEANUTS AND LIME

SERVES 2

GF

2 whole mackerel
(150–200g each), cleaned,
gutted and bloodline removed

1 tablespoons vegetable oil

1 teaspoon coarse sea salt

100g caster sugar

1 teaspoon table salt

100ml distilled white vinegar

60g bean sprouts

5g dill, chopped

10g coriander leaves,
chopped

10g Thai sweet basil
(or Italian basil), torn

2 green bird's-eye chillies,
thinly sliced

2 tablespoons roasted
peanuts, lightly crushed

2 tablespoons chilli oil

steamed jasmine rice,
to serve

Grilled mackerel is something that I have become increasingly fond of over the past few years. Its oily flesh and skin make it such a wonderful thing to barbecue and eat. Literally, just a sprinkle of salt on top of a good quality mackerel is enough to impress. As with sardines, I think it's always nice to put it with something both textural and a little sharp, to work in harmony with its richness. Pickled bean sprouts are perfect for this, being light, crunchy and flavoursome.

Light the barbecue to a high heat. Using your hands, rub the vegetable oil into the mackerel skin, then sprinkle with the coarse sea salt. Place the fish on a grill directly over red-hot embers and cook for 6–8 minutes on each side until the skin is golden brown and crispy and the flesh is cooked all the way through (for best results, use a temperature probe and take the fish off the barbecue when it reaches 65–68°C), leaving it to rest for 3 minutes before serving. The fish should be about 70°C after resting as it continues to cook.

Meanwhile, pickle the bean sprouts. In a medium saucepan, heat the sugar, table salt, vinegar and 100ml cold water, then remove from the heat, add the bean sprouts and allow to cool. The heat from the pickling juice will penetrate the bean sprouts fully. Once cool, drain the bean sprouts, transfer them to a large mixing bowl along with the dill, coriander, basil, chillies, peanuts and chilli oil, and toss well. Serve the mackerel on top of the bean sprouts, accompanied with steamed jasmine rice.

SERVES 2
AS A SIDE

200g cherry tomatoes

2 large beef tomatoes, sliced into 8 chunks

100g green tomatoes

2 long red chillies, stems removed

1 tablespoon palm sugar (or soft dark brown sugar)

2 limes (1 juiced and 1 diced)

juice of 1 clementine

50ml soy sauce

1 teaspoon caster sugar

1 stick lemongrass, outer layer removed and very thinly sliced

3 spring onions, thinly sliced

50ml vegetable stock

15g coriander leaves, roughly torn

15g mint leaves, roughly torn

1 teaspoon sesame oil

3 tablespoons sliced Thai shallots (or banana shallots)

salt and freshly ground black pepper

BLISTERED TOMATO
AND LIME SALAD

Always store your tomatoes in a fruit bowl, never the fridge – a pet hate of mine for years! Tomatoes are porous, and take on the flavours of the things around them, so if you put them in the fridge they'll end up tasting like your Camembert. It's of particular importance in this recipe, where the flavour of the tomatoes is crucial. By blistering them on the barbecue, they take on a smoky flavour that turns this simple salad into something truly amazing.

This is great as a side salad with meat and fish, but if you want to make it a main meal, serve with some rice.

First, grill all the tomatoes and the chillies on the barbecue. Ideally, this should be done over a wood fire, but if you have an electric or gas barbecue they will still take on a smoky flavour. Place them onto direct heat and cook for about 5 minutes on each side until they are blistered and charred all over and have softened slightly. As soon as they are cooked, put them straight into a mixing bowl so no juices are lost, as this all contributes to the salad dressing. Stir in the sugar immediately, so that it melts.

Next, add the lime and clementine juices and soy sauce to the bowl. Stir, taste and season a little if needed – it should be sweet, salty, sour and smoky.

Finally, add all the remaining ingredients, delicately toss together and serve immediately.

SERVES 2

4 Thai purple aubergines
(or regular aubergines)

2 duck eggs

10g jasmine rice

10g mint, torn

10g coriander, torn

10g Thai shallots,
peeled and thinly sliced
(or banana shallots)

1 teaspoon toasted sesame
seeds, to garnish

FOR THE PICKLE

2 tablespoons caster sugar

½ teaspoon table salt

50ml distilled white vinegar

¼ cucumber, thinly sliced

FOR THE DRESSING

juice of 5 limes

juice of 1 mandarin
(or clementine)

3 teaspoons fish sauce
(or soy sauce)

½ teaspoon chilli powder

50g caster sugar

3 teaspoons tamarind water

SMOKY
AUBERGINE SALAD
with RUNNY DUCK EGGS

When cooked over an open fire, aubergine transforms into a smoky, soft bombshell of taste. I've used Thai purple aubergines, which are thinner and easier to grill evenly in a short time. You can also use ordinary aubergines, but they may need a little longer on the fire. And if you want, you can make the dish without a barbecue and still get tasty results.

Light the barbecue and place the whole aubergines directly onto the hot coals, or near the hottest part of the grill if you're using a gas barbecue. Turn them over frequently, ensuring that the heat from the coals is distributed evenly. The aubergines are ready when they are soft to the touch, with charred, blistered skins. When cool enough to handle, peel off the skin. (If you are not using a barbecue, crank the oven right up to full blast and bake the aubergines until the skins are charred and the flesh is soft – this will take 20–25 minutes).

Meanwhile, cook the duck eggs for 6–7 minutes on a rolling boil in salted water, then transfer into a bowl of ice-cold water with a splash of olive oil. If you peel the eggs in the water, the oil gets between the shell and the flesh, making them easier to peel.

Put the rice in a dry frying pan and lightly toast on a medium heat, shaking the pan constantly until the grains have turned golden brown. Pound the rice into a powder in a granite pestle and mortar, or use a spice grinder. Be sure to grind the rice to a powder as it will be used to add texture to the salad; it will be too crunchy if the grains are too coarse.

Next, make the pickle. In a medium saucepan, gently heat the sugar, salt and vinegar together with 50ml cold water until the sugar has dissolved. Be sure to keep stirring so that the sugar dissolves without heating the water too much. Remove from the heat and add the cucumber, then refrigerate.

Now make the dressing. In a bowl, mix the lime and mandarin juices, the fish sauce, chilli powder, sugar and tamarind water. Taste and adjust the dressing to suit your own taste buds: it should be sweet, salty, sour and hot, with an edge towards the salt and citrus. When you're happy with the flavour, add the aubergines, mint, coriander, shallots and the pickled cucumber (straining any pickling juices before adding), then gently fold together, leaving the aubergines whole if you can be delicate enough.

Arrange the aubergines on a serving plate and place the duck eggs on top. Using the tip of a knife, pierce a hole in the eggs and break them open with your fingers, releasing the runny yolks so that they ooze into the salad. Sprinkle the salad with the rice and sesame seeds and add a tiny pinch of salt onto the runny egg yolks as a surprise burst of flavour. Serve with steamed jasmine rice for an extra fill.

SERVES 2

ROASTED PEACH MASSAMAN ᴡɪᴛʜ ASIAN VEGETABLES, PEANUTS ᴀɴᴅ CORIANDER

100ml vegetable oil, plus a
little to brush the peaches

100g massaman curry paste
(see page 162)

20g unsalted roasted peanuts,
plus 5g chopped, to garnish

2 tablespoons palm sugar
(or soft dark brown sugar)

50ml soy sauce (or fish sauce)

300ml hot vegetable stock

400ml coconut cream

150g new potatoes, halved

50g baby sweetcorn, halved
lengthways

¼ small pineapple, peeled
and roughly diced

50g green beans, topped and
tailed and cut in half

10g Thai sweet basil
(or Italian basil), torn

2 peaches, halved and stoned

a pinch of table salt

a pinch of caster sugar

steamed jasmine rice,
to serve

10g coriander leaves, torn,
to garnish

**Traditionally, massaman curry is cooked with beef, chicken
or mutton, but the curry paste, which is heavily packed with
aromatic dry spices, is also delicious with sweet and acidic
fresh fruit.**

Pour the oil into a large, non-stick pan and place over a medium heat.
Add the massaman curry paste and fry, stirring and scraping constantly
using a flat-headed metal spoon to prevent the paste sticking to the
bottom of the pan. After a few minutes, add the peanuts and fry for
a further 15 minutes or so until the paste starts to darken and the
mixture smells of one thing rather than individual components.

Add the sugar and fry for a few minutes until it dissolves and begins
to caramelise – you will know when this happens as the paste will darken
further. At this stage, add the soy sauce, vegetable stock and half the
coconut cream, and reduce the heat to allow the curry to simmer and
the flavours to infuse. Add the potatoes and allow to gently simmer in the
curry for about 10 minutes, then add the sweetcorn, pineapple and green
beans and simmer for a further 8–10 minutes until all the vegetables have
reached the desired softness. Throw in the basil and the remaining coconut
cream just before serving.

Meanwhile, preheat the oven to 200°C/gas mark 6. Brush a little oil
onto the cut surface of the peaches and sprinkle with a pinch of salt and
sugar. Place on a baking tray lined with baking parchment and roast in the
oven for 20 minutes until golden brown and softened. Remove and keep
warm. Alternatively, (and preferable to me) brush the peaches with oil and
barbecue them until soft and charred, then sprinkle with sugar and salt just
before taking them off the heat.

Serve the peaches on top of the rice. Spoon over a large ladleful of
curry, sprinkle with the coriander and garnish with some chopped peanuts.

SERVES 4

4 large chicken legs on
the bone (about 150g each),
trimmed

150g caster sugar

300g table salt

5 kaffir lime leaves, torn

2 pandan leaves, tied in a knot

1kg ice

100g desiccated coconut

1 teaspoon smoked chilli
powder

sticky glutinous rice,
to serve (optional)

FOR THE MARINADE

2 tablespoons chopped
coriander roots

8 garlic cloves, peeled

10g galangal, peeled and
roughly chopped (or ginger)

½ teaspoon coarse sea salt

150ml kecap manis

30ml fish sauce

2 tablespoons dark soy sauce

50g palm sugar (or soft
brown sugar)

2 tablespoons toasted whole
coriander seeds, bruised

1 tablespoon sesame oil

STICKY BARBECUE CHICKEN

Known in Thailand as *gai yang*, this is another incredibly popular dish that traditionally is grilled over an open fire and served with sticky glutinous rice and a spicy *som tam* salad. At Farang, we always brine our chicken before barbecuing as this allows the meat to absorb flavour and moisture, meaning it can be cooked on a high heat without the worry of it overcooking or drying out.

First, get the chicken legs brining: in a large saucepan bring 2 litres of water to a simmer and then dissolve the sugar and table salt in the water. Add the kaffir lime leaves and the pandan leaves and leave to infuse for a few minutes, then remove from the heat and tip in the ice to cool the mixture quickly. Once cool, submerge the chicken legs in the brine and refrigerate for 2 hours. Remove the legs from the brine and pat dry with a clean kitchen towel, then discard the brining liquid.

Meanwhile, make the marinade. Pound the coriander roots, garlic and galangal to a paste in a pestle and mortar or food processor, using the sea salt as an abrasive. In a medium non-stick saucepan, add the kecap manis, fish sauce, dark soy sauce, palm sugar, coriander seeds, sesame oil and the paste. Cook, stirring constantly, until all the ingredients have melded together to make a sauce. Remove from the heat, allow to cool, then place the chicken legs into this sauce and leave to marinate for a minimum of 1 hour, but preferably overnight.

If using a barbecue, grill the chicken over hot embers, skin-side up. This allows the skin to dry out so it crisps up better when you flip the legs over. Grill the chicken legs for 8–10 minutes on either side, constantly tossing small amounts of the desiccated coconut onto the embers underneath the chicken to add a little smoke flavour to the meat. The chicken is ready when the outside is crisp, charred and caramelised, and the inside is piping hot. Make a small incision with the tip of a sharp knife all the way to the bone – if the meat is still a little pink, cook for a few more minutes. For best results, use a temperature probe and take the chicken off the barbecue when the core temperature reaches 66–68°C, then rest for 5 minutes before serving.

Meanwhile, bring the leftover marinade to the boil and simmer for 5 minutes until all the sugars have caramelised and the sauce has thickened slightly. Taste for seasoning: it should be sweet and salty, so adjust if necessary.

Use a cleaver to chop the chicken into bite-sized pieces and serve drizzled with the sauce and dusted with the smoked chilli powder. For a proper feed, serve with sticky glutinous rice to mop up the excess juices.

GRILLED SEA BREAM

WITH SWEET AND SOUR CHILLI SAUCE

SERVES 2   GF
                              OPTIONAL

2 sea bream (150–200g each),
scored, scaled, cleaned and
gutted, bloodline removed

4 sticks of lemongrass,
bruised

4 kaffir lime leaves, torn

2 pandan leaves, tied in knots

3 large 40 x 60cm banana
leaves

I lime, cut into wedges

sticky glutinous rice,
to serve

FOR THE SAUCE

20g ginger, peeled and
chopped

4 tablespoons finely chopped
coriander roots

8 garlic cloves, peeled

2 teaspoons coarse sea salt

8 long red chillies, sliced
into rounds

8 long green chillies, sliced
into rounds

3 tablespoons vegetable oil,
plus extra for greasing

4 tablespoons soy sauce
(or fish sauce)

100g palm sugar

100ml hot vegetable stock

4 tablespoons thick
tamarind water

This dish is usually made by deep-frying the fish and pouring the sauce over at the end. However, I prefer to grill the fish, as this means the flesh remains moist and retains all its natural flavours. If grilled correctly, it is possible to have crispy fish skin with a sticky sauce over the top.

Pound the ginger, coriander roots and garlic to a coarse paste in a pestle and mortar, using the salt as an abrasive. Transfer to a small bowl then, in the same mortar, bruise the chillies to release their flavour and soften them.

Meanwhile, heat the oil to a high heat in a large frying pan and fry the paste, stirring it constantly to avoid it sticking to the pan. When it begins to darken, add the bruised chillies and fry for a further minute to soften. Add the soy sauce, palm sugar and vegetable stock and simmer until the sugar has melted and the ingredients combine to become a thick sauce. Finally, add the tamarind water and set aside. The sauce should be shiny and thick and taste sweet, salty, sour and hot.

Light the barbecue and get the coals glowing red, ready for grilling the sea bream. Stuff each fish with 2 lemongrass sticks, 2 lime leaves and I pandan leaf, and season with a good pinch of salt. Coat the outside of the fish with a pinch of salt and a light gloss of oil. Place the banana leaves over the hot flames and then place a fish on each leaf. Grill for 6–8 minutes until the skin begins to turn golden brown, then turn the fish over, baste the fish a little in the sauce so that it cooks into the fish and grill for a further 6–8 minutes. For best results, use a temperature probe and take the fish off the barbecue when it reaches 65–68°C, then leave to rest for 3 minutes before serving. The fish should be about 70°C after resting as it continues to cook.

Serve the fish on the grilled banana leaves with the remaining sauce drizzled over. If you want to impress your friends, top with some fried, crispy kaffir lime leaves and a wedge of lime. Serve with sticky glutinous rice to mop up all the sauce.

SERVES 2

3 40 x 60cm banana leaves

I sea bass (250–300g), cleaned, gutted and scaled with bloodline removed

10g Thai sweet basil, chopped

4 cocktail sticks

10g ginger, peeled and julienne

10g coriander, finely chopped

sticky rice, to serve (optional)

FOR THE SAUCE

150g crispy chilli and coconut jam (see page 161)

2 teaspoons fish sauce

I teaspoon thick tamarind water

80ml coconut cream

WHOLE SEA BASS
WITH COCONUT CHILLI JAM
AND FRESH HERBS

Before I began to cook Thai food I trained in British/ European cuisine and grew up in kitchens around where I lived in Oxfordshire. At this stage in my career, I always thought of chilli jam as one entity, involving a similar process to most regular jams. The Thais, however, have made chilli jam a wondrous and plentiful thing; there are four different types that I know of, so far. Referred to in Thailand as *nam prik pao*, this flavoursome combination of carefully fried ingredients works amazingly as a marinade when combined with a little coconut cream. The banana leaves add flavour and aid in the grilling process, protecting the fish from the naked flames. However, if you can't find them, use foil.

In a small saucepan, gently heat the chilli jam over a low heat, being mindful not to heat it too aggressively as the jam ingredients have already been fried. Add the fish sauce, tamarind water and coconut cream, then remove from the heat and allow to cool.

On a flat surface, lay two banana leaves on top of each other, then lay the final leaf with the grain of the leaf facing the opposite way as this will give strength to the parcel. Place the sea bass in the centre of the banana leaves and pour two-thirds of the coconut jam mixture over the top and use your hands to rub it all over the fish, then put half the basil leaves on top. Carefully wrap the banana leaves around the fish to make a rectangular parcel, then use the cocktail sticks to secure the corners.

Place the sea bass parcel over hot embers and barbecue for 6–8 minutes on each side until the fish skin is charred and the flesh is cooked. For best results, use a temperature probe and take the fish off the barbecue when it reaches 65–68°C, then leave to rest for 3 minutes before serving. The fish should be about 70°C after resting as it continues to cook.

Unwrap the parcel and serve the seabass scattered with the ginger, coriander and remaining basil and, if you have any left from making the jam, some crispy garlic, chilli, shrimp and shallots. For a bigger meal, eat accompanied with sticky rice to mop up all the juices.

4 CURRIES & BIG ONES

RED CURRY OF POUSSIN
AND MINCED PRAWNS WITH
ASIAN VEGETABLES

50g prawns, shells and heads removed and deveined, minced using a meat cleaver (save the heads and shells)

I teaspoon sea salt

150ml coconut oil
(or vegetable oil)

200g red curry paste
(see page 163)

I tablespoon palm sugar

2–3 tablespoons fish sauce, to taste

200ml coconut cream

I poussin (about 250–300g)

20g white daikon, peeled and sliced into thin rounds and blanched in water until soft (optional)

20g green beans, topped and tailed, cut into 2cm pieces

20g baby sweetcorn, thinly sliced

10g Thai basil, plus a little extra, to garnish

2 long red chillies, sliced into rounds

2 long green chillies, sliced into rounds

2 tablespoons wild ginger (*krachai*), peeled and thinly sliced (or regular ginger)

10g coriander, to garnish

steamed jasmine rice, to serve

This is a simple way to infuse chicken with the flavours of red curry. I've always used baby chickens, as they are perfect for sharing between two, but it works just as well with larger chickens, if you adjust the cooking times to suit. You can also leave the chicken to marinate in the red curry paste overnight before roasting, to enhance the flavour.

Bring the prawn heads and shells to the boil in 300ml water with the salt, then reduce the heat, skim off the scum, simmer for 20 minutes, then strain the light prawn stock into a bowl.

Heat the coconut oil in a wok, add the red curry paste and keep stirring and scraping until it begins to split like scrambled eggs. The smell of the ingredients will also change from raw to fragrant. I find that as you cook out curry pastes you can smell each ingredient cooking at different times – I assume this is based on the water content of each vegetable – and eventually the smell becomes one, which is a sign that it is ready. At this point, stir in the palm sugar and cook for a further minute until the paste has darkened slightly, then add 2 tablespoons of the fish sauce and cook for 1 minute; don't add too much fish sauce as it is strong and you can always add but never take away.

Add 200ml of the prawn stock and 100ml of the coconut cream. Now remove half this curry paste from the pan and allow it to cool, then thoroughly coat the chicken in it and leave it to marinate, ideally overnight (or you can cook it straight away if you're short of time).

Preheat the oven to 220°C/gas mark 7. Roast the chicken for 35–40 minutes until the skin is crispy, the marinade has become slightly charred and the juices run clear. Allow it to rest for 10 minutes before serving.

Meanwhile, bring your attention back to the rest of the cooked-out curry paste. Bring this back to a simmer, then add the daikon, green beans and baby sweetcorn. Stir to combine, then cover and bring to a simmer. Cook for about 5 minutes until all the vegetables are cooked. At this point, the curry will have thickened a little, so add the remaining prawn stock and coconut cream and the minced prawns. Cook for 3 minutes until the prawns are pink and cooked through. Next, fold in the basil, red and green chillies, fish sauce to taste and wild ginger. The curry should be spicy, creamy, aromatic, sweet, fishy and salty all at the same time, but adjust it to suit you.

Serve the chicken whole with the prawn and vegetable curry over the top and, if you like, a few sprigs of basil and coriander for decoration. Delicious with steamed jasmine rice.

AROMATIC BEEF BRAISED IN COCONUT CREAM AND GINGER

400g beef shin, excess fat removed and chopped into 3cm chunks

50ml good-quality olive oil

1 tablespoon coarse sea salt

2 sticks lemongrass, bruised

4 kaffir lime leaves, torn

2 long red chillies, bruised

15g Thai shallots, peeled and left whole (or any small, sweet shallot)

20g ginger, peeled and fine julienned

600–700ml coconut cream (enough to submerge the beef)

1 heaped tablespoon of tamarind paste

20–25ml fish sauce

1 heaped tablespoon soft brown sugar

10g coriander leaves, torn, to garnish

10g Thai sweet basil (or Italian basil), torn, to garnish

steamed jasmine rice, to serve

There is nothing more appealing to the home cook than a one-pot wonder, especially on a cold winter's day when you need something simple that warms the soul! Using coconut cream and fish sauce instead of stock and salt to braise beef produces some seriously amazing results. The trick to this dish is low and slow; let the heat of the oven do all the work.

Massage the olive oil and salt into the beef with your hands to ensure all the meat gets a good coating.

Preheat the oven to 140°C/gas mark 1. In a large ovenproof tray, add the beef, lemongrass, kaffir lime leaves, long red chillies, Thai shallots, two-thirds of the ginger, the coconut cream, tamarind paste, fish sauce and sugar. Check all the ingredients are completely submerged in the coconut cream, then tightly wrap the tray in foil to protect the contents from the direct heat of the oven. Place the tray on the middle shelf of the oven and cook for 5–6 hours.

Check the beef is cooked properly – you should be able to break up the pieces of meat with a spoon it is so tender. When you are satisfied the beef is ready, taste the coconut broth to ensure you are happy with the seasoning. It should be delicately sweet from the coconut cream and moreishly salty from the fish sauce. Add a little more of either if you think necessary.

Serve the stew in bowls topped with the remaining ginger and the coriander and basil. This dish is great served with steamed jasmine rice.

CURRIED CRAB CLAWS WITH FENNEL AND FRESH HERBS

2 tablespoons table salt

I fennel bulb, core removed and chopped into 8 long chunks

600–800g crab claws

100ml coconut oil
(or vegetable oil)

150g yellow curry paste
(see page 163)

30g yellow bean paste

2 tablespoons palm sugar

3 tablespoons light soy sauce

100ml hot fish stock

3 tablespoons thick tamarind water

30g brown crab meat

250ml coconut cream

10g Thai sweet basil
(or Italian basil)

10g coriander leaves, torn, to garnish

I teaspoon chilli powder, to garnish

I lime, cut into wedges

There is nothing better in life than serving people with a plate of food that is too delicious to resist, but impossible to eat without making a complete mess of themselves! This needs to be served with lots of napkins and finger bowls, otherwise you'd better sit everyone outside to protect the walls and ceilings from a crab attack. I like to share this with a large group of friends, accompanied with steamed jasmine rice.

In a large saucepan, bring some water to a simmer with the salt. Blanch the fennel for 3 minutes until softened, then remove it from the pan and set aside. Now go straight in with the crab claws and simmer for 3 minutes to part-cook them. Remove them from the water and set aside to cool slightly. When cool enough to handle, gently tap each claw with a pestle or rolling pin to crack open the claw and allow easy access for your diners.

In a large non-stick wok or pan, heat the coconut oil until it is bubbling and sizzling. Add the yellow curry paste and the yellow bean paste to the pan and fry for 6–8 minutes, stirring all the time, until the paste begins to darken, then add the palm sugar and cook for a further minute or so until the sugar has begun to caramelise and the paste darkens a little more. At this point, deglaze the pan with the soy sauce and add the fish stock, tamarind water, crab meat, 200ml of the coconut cream, the blanched fennel and the crab claws. Cover with a lid and simmer for 2–3 minutes until the crab claws are cooked through and the fennel has softened a little more. At this point, the curry should taste sweet, salty and fishy; the sourness and spiciness are added with the garnish.

Stir in the basil leaves and remaining coconut cream, then serve in a big pile topped with the coriander, chilli powder and lime wedges, accompanied by steamed jasmine rice and finger bowls.

SERVES 2

MASSAMAN CURRY OF PALM SUGAR-BRAISED QUINCE

1 teaspoon table salt

120g palm sugar (or soft dark brown sugar)

2 quinces, halved and cored

100ml vegetable oil

100g massaman curry paste (see page 162)

20g unsalted roasted peanuts, plus 5g chopped to serve

50ml soy sauce (or fish sauce)

300ml hot vegetable stock

400ml coconut cream

150g new potatoes, halved

50g baby sweetcorn, chopped in half lengthways

¼ small pineapple, peeled and roughly diced

50g green beans, topped and tailed and cut in half

10g Thai sweet basil (or Italian basil), torn

10g coriander leaves, torn, to garnish

steamed jasmine rice, to serve

This is another awesome take on a traditional massaman curry. Once again, I've kept it vegetarian and packed it full of fresh fruits and Asian vegetables, as for me they make the perfect pairing with the aromatic spices. Quince is a personal favourite of mine and, when poached slowly in palm sugar syrup on a low heat, they turn an amazing ruby red colour, whilst still keeping a meaty texture. The leftover quince syrup is lovely in mulled wine, desserts or cocktails.

In a large saucepan, bring 1 litre water to a simmer with the salt and 100g of the palm sugar, stirring occasionally until the sugar has dissolved. Add the quinces, cover with parchment paper and simmer for 2–3 hours until the quinces are ruby red and softened, then remove them from the pan and set aside. Reserve the liquid for use later.

Pour the oil into a large non-stick frying pan and place over a medium heat. Fry the massaman curry paste, stirring and scraping constantly to prevent the paste sticking to the bottom of the pan. After a few minutes, add the peanuts and fry for a further 15 minutes or so until the paste starts to darken and the mixture smells fragrant.

Add the remaining palm sugar and fry for a few minutes until it dissolves and begins to caramelise and the paste darkens further. Add the soy sauce, vegetable stock and half the coconut cream, and reduce the heat to allow the curry to simmer and the flavours to infuse. Add the potatoes and gently simmer in the curry for about 10 minutes, then add the sweetcorn, pineapple and green beans, and simmer for a further 8–10 minutes until all the vegetables have softened but retain a little crunch. Throw in the basil, quinces and remaining coconut cream just before serving. The curry should be sweet, aromatic and savoury; if it's too sweet, add a little more soy sauce to balance the flavours, if too salty add some of the leftover quince braising juice.

Serve the curry in bowls, topped with the chopped peanuts and coriander, accompanied with steamed jasmine rice.

200g beef cheeks, trimmed

2 sticks lemongrass, bruised

20g galangal, bruised

4 kaffir lime leaves, torn

4 banana shallots, cut in half

2 tablespoons table salt

I head of garlic, sliced in half across the cloves

2 tablespoons finely chopped coriander roots

2 tablespoons wild ginger (*krachai*), peeled and roughly chopped (or regular ginger)

4 garlic cloves, peeled

½ tablespoon coarse sea salt

2 tablespoons vegetable oil

100g jungle curry paste (see page 163)

I tablespoon caster sugar

2 tablespoons fish sauce

30g new potatoes, cut in half

I pak choi, core removed and chopped into bite-sized pieces

30g green beans

10g hot Vietnamese mint, torn (optional)

10g betel leaves (or spinach)

10g coriander, torn

10g Thai sweet basil (or Italian basil), torn

10g fresh curry leaves

JUNGLE CURRY OF BEEF CHEEKS, GREEN PEPPERCORNS AND SWEET BASIL

Originating from the forested regions of Northern Thailand, jungle curry has a very distinctive flavour. It's fried in two stages and then boiled to achieve good depth of flavour, and it is often made with boar or river fish, both of which are delicious. However, my absolute favourite is a slow-cook cut of beef (you can use whatever cut you like), as the stock created from braising the meat produces remarkable results. Handfuls of fresh herbs also help make this curry something incredibly special.

Start by braising the beef cheeks. Preheat the oven to 100°C/gas mark ¼. In a large ovenproof casserole dish, submerge the beef cheeks in cold water, then add the lemongrass, galangal, kaffir lime leaves, shallots, table salt and garlic head. Cover the surface of the liquid with parchment paper and the pan with foil to protect the contents from the direct heat of the oven, and cook for 8 hours (this is best cooked overnight). Check the beef cheeks are cooked properly; they should be so tender you can cut them with a spoon. Remove the casserole from the oven and set aside.

In a pestle and mortar, pound the coriander roots, ginger and garlic cloves to a paste, using the coarse sea salt as an abrasive. Next, heat the vegetable oil in a wok or non-stick pan, then fry out the paste, scraping and stirring constantly. When the paste begins to darken slightly, add the jungle curry paste and continue to cook, stirring, making sure it doesn't stick and burn. Now add the kaffir lime leaves and the lemongrass from the beef braising stock. Continue to fry the paste until it begins to darken, then add the sugar and fry for a further minute until the sugar has caramelised and the paste has darkened a little more.

Deglaze the pan with the fish sauce and 300ml of beef braising stock. Bring to a simmer, then add the potatoes and cook for 10 minutes until they begin to soften. Add the pak choi, green beans and beef cheeks and, using a little more braising stock if needed, continue to simmer until all ingredients have softened.

Finally, add all the herbs and gently toss them through the hot curry, which should be loose, yet rich and spicy with a salty edge. Serve immediately in bowls with steamed jasmine rice, and top with crispy garlic and shallots, if you like.

SMOKY GREEN CURRY BROTH OF MONKFISH AND HERBS WITH VERMICELLI RICE NOODLES

SERVES 2-3   GF

- 150ml coconut oil
- 150g green curry paste
- 1 teaspoon palm sugar
- 200ml hot fish stock
- 250ml coconut cream
- 20g white daikon, peeled and sliced into thin rounds and braised in water for 5 minutes until softened
- 10g green beans, topped, tailed and cut into 2cm pieces
- 20g baby sweetcorn, sliced into thin rounds
- 200g monkfish tails
- 2 tablespoons fish sauce
- 10g Thai sweet basil, torn
- 3 long green chillies, sliced into rounds
- 3 long red chillies, sliced into rounds
- 1 tablespoon wild ginger (*krachai*), peeled and thinly sliced (or regular ginger)
- 150g fine vermicelli rice noodles, blanched for 1 minute in boiling salted water and then refreshed in cold water
- 10g coriander, chopped, to garnish
- 1 lime, cut into wedges, to serve

This is another example of how versatile green curry is. Here it's loosened to the point where it is almost a soup and served with noodles and monkfish. Although it'd also be delicious with most seafood or chicken, I prefer using white fish, as it cooks so delicately and easily when dropped into a gently simmering broth.

Heat the coconut oil in a wok. When bubbling, add the green curry paste and keep stirring and scraping regularly until the paste begins to split like scrambled eggs and darkens slightly. You will notice that the smell changes from raw to fragrant as all the ingredients cook together. Add the palm sugar and cook for 1 minute until the paste darkens a little more as the sugar caramelises.

Add the fish stock and half the coconut cream, the daikon, green beans and baby sweetcorn. Stir to combine, then cover and simmer for about 5 minutes until the vegetables are cooked.

Drop in the monkfish tails and cover with the lid. Simmer for 3–4 minutes until the fish is cooked through. At this point, the curry will have thickened a little, so add the remaining coconut cream and the fish sauce. Add the basil, green and red chillies, a little more fish sauce to taste (if you like) and the wild ginger. Fold these ingredients in carefully as you don't want to break up the fish.

Place portions of the cooked noodles in bowls, then ladle the curry over the top. The curry should be rich, creamy, salty, hot and fishy, and thick enough to coat the noodles. The magic is in the balance of flavours. Top with coriander and lime.

SMOKED SALMON LAKSA
WITH SOFT-BOILED EGGS

100ml vegetable oil

300g roasted red curry paste
(see page 166)

1 tablespoon mild curry
powder

10g dried shrimp, ground
to a floss

2 medium eggs

1 tablespoon soft
brown sugar

2 tablespoons fish sauce

200ml hot fish stock

400ml coconut cream

400g smoked salmon fillets,
cut into bite-sized pieces

300g fine vermicelli rice
noodles, blanched for
1 minute in boiling salted
water and then refreshed
in cold water

10g coriander, chopped,
to garnish

3 tablespoons toasted
peanuts, lightly crushed

20g pickled mustard greens,
chopped (optional), to garnish

1 large lime, cut into
3 wedges, to serve

The *laksa* is originally from Indonesia but is widely accepted to be a result of the mixing of cultures and cooking practices in Chinese coastal settlements. Its popularity has led to variations being developed in Malaysia, Singapore and, most importantly for me, southern Thailand. The dish offers the characteristics of a curry and a soup, making it ideal to eat with noodles as a way of soaking up all the delicious juices.

Heat the oil in a medium saucepan. When sizzling hot, add the curry paste, curry powder and shrimp, and fry while shaking the pan and scraping regularly to ensure the mixture doesn't stick. Cook for 8–10 minutes until all the ingredients come together and the paste looks a little darker.

Meanwhile, soft-boil and then peel the eggs: a medium-size egg takes 5 minutes to soft-boil on a rolling boil. I always cook mine in salted water and then put them into a bowl of ice-cold water with a splash of olive oil. If you peel the eggs in the water, the oil gets between the shell and the flesh, making them easier to peel. Set the eggs aside.

Back to the paste: add the sugar and cook for a few minutes until the paste darkens a little more as the sugar caramelises. Deglaze the pan by adding the fish sauce and the fish stock, then bring back to the boil. Add the coconut cream and bring to a simmer. Check the seasoning as you may prefer a little more sugar or fish sauce.

Drop the salmon into the curry and stir for 1–2 minutes. The residual heat from the curry will heat it very quickly. Serve in a large bowl with the blanched noodles. Pour the hot curry over the noodles to warm them up. Garnish with a sprinkling of coriander, the peanuts, the pickled mustard greens, the eggs cut in half with the soft yolks running into the curry, and wedges of lime to squeeze over.

SERVES 2-3

SWEET SOY-INFUSED STICKY PORK RIBS WITH CHILLI, LIME LEAVES AND FRESH HERBS

300ml kecap manis
(Indonesian sweet soy sauce)

I stick lemongrass, outer
sheath removed and core
sliced wafer thin

2 kaffir lime leaves, stems
removed and julienned

2 long red chillies, stems
removed and thinly sliced

2 long green chillies, stems
removed and thinly sliced

4 green bird's-eye chillies,
thinly sliced

2 tablespoons cumin seeds,
ground to a powder

2 tablespoons white
peppercorns, ground to
a powder

4 banana shallots, peeled and
thinly sliced

5 garlic cloves, peeled and
thinly sliced

50ml fish sauce

I rack of pork ribs

I lime, cut into wedges,
to serve

10g coriander, chopped,
to garnish

If I was told that the world was going to end tomorrow, I would have only one thing on my mind – 'Shit! What am I going to eat for dinner?' One of the contenders would have to be these sticky ribs, and as pork is the most widely eaten meat in the world, I'm sure I wouldn't be alone in thinking this recipe worthy of a last supper. The beauty of cooking ribs in this way is that it takes mere minutes to throw together so all you need to do is wait for the magic to happen in the oven. They can be slow cooked over a barbecue, too, if you fancy giving it a try.

In a large bowl, make the marinade by combining the kecap manis, lemongrass, kaffir lime leaves, chillies, cumin seeds, white peppercorns, shallots, garlic and fish sauce. Coat the pork ribs in the marinade, using your hands to rub it all over the meat. Refrigerate and leave to marinate for a minimum of 2 hours, but ideally overnight.

Preheat the oven to 140°C/gas mark 1. To cook the ribs, tightly wrap them in foil with all the marinade locked inside and place the parcel on a roasting tray in the oven for 3–4 hours until the meat is tender and falls off the bone.

If you are barbecuing, the ribs can be taken straight out of the oven and placed on the barbecue grill to colour, basting regularly with any leftover marinade. Otherwise, place the ribs on a plate and garnish with the lime wedges and coriander. These ribs are great served with steamed jasmine rice.

TIPS

Kecap manis is a great
addition to any Thai
cook's kitchen. It's a
sweet Indonesian soy
sauce with a thick, black
treacle, molasses-like
consistency. It's ideal
as a quick marinade for
Barbecued meat and fish
and is also commonly
used in dipping sauces
for added richness and
depth of flavour.

MINCED CURRIED BEEF AND TURMERIC BUTTER ROTIS

SERVES 2–3   GF

125g plain flour, sifted

I teaspoon coriander seeds, toasted and lightly bruised

I small egg, beaten

100ml warm water

3 tablespoons olive oil

150g unsalted butter

3cm fresh red turmeric, peeled and left whole (or ½ teaspoon dried turmeric)

4 red bird's-eye chillies, stems removed

I tablespoon coriander roots (optional)

I tablespoon fresh red turmeric, peeled and roughly chopped (or ½ teaspoon dried turmeric)

6 garlic cloves, peeled

20g ginger, peeled and roughly chopped

a pinch of coarse sea salt

250g beef mince

I teaspoon caster sugar

10g coriander leaves, chopped

20g Thai shallots, peeled and sliced (or banana shallots)

juice of ½ lime

2 tablespoons fish sauce

Roti parcels come in all shapes and sizes with different kinds of sweet and savoury fillings. This is one of my favourites. It's best to use chuck steak as it is roughly 20 per cent fat, which contributes hugely to the flavour.

Start by making the roti dough. Place the flour and coriander seeds in a bowl, make a well in the centre, add the egg and rub together until the mixture is the consistency of breadcrumbs. Gradually add the water, then knead for 8–10 minutes. The dough should be tacky but not sticking to the bowl or your fingers. If it's too wet add a little flour; if it's too dry add a little water, but bear in mind it should be quite wet compared to regular bread dough. Place the dough in a lightly oiled bowl and cover with clingfilm, making sure the clingfilm is in direct contact with the dough to stop it crusting over. Leave to rest for a minimum of 30 minutes.

Meanwhile, gently melt the butter in a small frying pan with the whole turmeric. Pour the clarified (clear) butter into a container and discard the fresh turmeric and sediment at the bottom.

In a pestle and mortar, pound the chillies, coriander root, turmeric, garlic and ginger to a paste using the salt as an abrasive, then cook in a large wok, placed over a high heat, scraping and stirring constantly until golden brown. Add the beef and fry until it is cooked through, then add the sugar and cook for a further minute until the mixture darkens and caramelises. Add the coriander, Thai shallots, lime juice and fish sauce, stir well and set aside.

Now for the fun bit. Lightly oil a clean surface. Pull off a chunk of dough and roll into a ball roughly the size of a ping pong ball. Repeat with the rest of the dough. Next, grab a ball and place it on the oiled surface. Flatten it into a rough circular shape, then gently lift the side closest to you and drag it towards you. Lift it quickly but delicately and slap it back onto the surface (because of the dough's elasticity it doesn't rip too easily and it stretches bigger as you drag it). Repeat until the dough is roughly 2–3mm thick (the thinner the better but don't make it too hard to lift into the pan – a few holes are fine). Alternatively, use a rolling pin, or just stretch the dough out with your hands. No one, including myself gets it perfect first time, so don't worry if it all goes a little pear shaped, it will still taste amazing.

Heat the clarified butter in a large frying pan over a medium heat (the butter needs to be hot to crisp the dough, but don't burn). Carefully, lift the dough circle into the pan; if it sizzles you're doing it right. Immediately place a large spoonful of the beef mince mixture into the centre of the roti and, using a pallet knife, carefully fold the roti dough into a rectangular parcel, wrapping the beef mix inside the parcel. Flip over to crisp the roti on the other side and then remove from the pan and drain on kitchen paper. Repeat with the remaining dough and beef mince. Sprinkle with a little coarse sea salt and then serve the rotis cut into triangles and piled up on a plate.

I large whole lobster
(300–400g)

40g ginger, peeled
and julienned

6 cloves garlic, peeled

2 red bird's-eye chillies,
stems removed

I tablespoon chopped
coriander roots (optional)

a pinch of coarse sea salt

2 tablespoons vegetable oil

25g fermented yellow
bean sauce, blitzed to
a smooth paste

3 tablespoons palm sugar
(or soft dark brown sugar)

400ml coconut cream

200g minced pork belly
(20% fat content)

a pinch of ground
white pepper

10g Thai sweet basil
(or Italian basil), torn

10g coriander leaves, torn

2 long red chillies,
sliced into rounds

20ml fish sauce

20ml tamarind water

FOR THE DIPPING VEGETABLES

I fennel bulb, chopped
into bite-sized chunks

I large cucumber,
sliced diagonally

100g green beans, topped
and tailed, and cooked in
boiling salted water for
a few minutes

I endive, separated
into leaves

MINCED PORK AND LOBSTER LON WITH DIPPING VEGETABLES

In Thailand, *lon* is served as a sharing snack or as part of a main meal. It usually comes as a loose, yet thick dip accompanied by raw vegetables, herbs and rice. This is surf 'n' turf at its finest, and is the absolute king of sharing plates. The fat in the pork helps to thicken the dip, so use a good-quality pork belly with some fat content. The lobster brain (tamale) is also key to this dish, so be sure not to discard anything.

Drop the lobster into boiling salted water and cook for 8 minutes, then carefully submerge into ice-cold water. Using a meat cleaver, chop the lobster in half lengthways, then discard the stomach sack and intestines, but separate and keep the tamale (this is located towards the head and is yellow/brown/orange in colour). Remove the flesh from the shell and roughly mince it using a meat cleaver. Do not discard the shell.

Now, make a light lobster stock. Place the lobster shell in a large saucepan, add 200ml water, bring to the boil, then remove from the heat and discard the shell.

Pound half the ginger with the garlic, bird's eye chillies and coriander roots (if using) to a coarse paste in a pestle and mortar, using the salt as an abrasive. Pour the oil into a separate large saucepan over a medium heat, add the paste and fry, constantly stirring and scraping until it is golden brown and smells fragrant; this will take about 2 minutes. Add the yellow bean sauce and fry for a further 5 minutes until it begins to darken further and starts to smell a little like miso. At this point, add the lobster tamale and two-thirds of the palm sugar. Fry gently for a further 2 minutes until all the ingredients are cooked.

Add all the lobster stock, 300ml of the coconut cream and the minced pork, then bring to a simmer. Be sure to break up the pork as it's cooking so it doesn't clump together. Simmer gently for 8–10 minutes until the pork is cooked through and the liquid has reduced to a thick scoopable consistency.

Add the minced lobster, white pepper, basil, coriander and remaining ginger and palm sugar, the chillies, fish sauce and tamarind water. Taste and adjust the seasoning before serving; the sauce should have a loose but dip-able consistency and be sweet, rich and salty. If necessary, loosen the *lon* with the remaining coconut cream.

Serve in a large serving bowl so people can help themselves, surrounded by the vegetables and, if you want, some steamed jasmine rice.

PORK SHANK BRAISED IN SWEET SOY

WITH EGGS AND NOODLES

1 pork shank (about 1.5kg), bone in

100ml vegetable oil

10 garlic cloves, peeled

3 tablespoons peeled and roughly chopped ginger

1 teaspoon ground white pepper

a pinch of coarse sea salt

1 litre hot chicken stock, plus extra if necessary

80ml fish sauce

2 tablespoons palm sugar (or soft dark brown sugar)

100ml sweet soy sauce

2 x 4cm pieces cassia bark (or 1 cinnamon stick)

2 fresh bay leaves (or dried)

100ml oyster sauce

4 medium eggs

150g fine vermicelli rice noodles, blanched in boiling salted water for 1 minute, then refreshed under cold water

10g coriander leaves, chopped, to garnish

This sweet, rich, aromatic stew is a lovely winter warmer. It's also all made in one pot, so can be thrown together in the morning and then left to braise all day. The pork is first roasted to allow the skin to crisp slightly and to melt the fat, which is then used to fry out a paste with spices and aromatics and let out with stock. The meat is then left to simmer for hours to create a shiny, porky broth that is quite extraordinary and beautiful eaten with rice noodles.

Preheat the oven to 180°C/gas mark 4. Rub the shank all over with a little oil and pour the remaining oil in a large cast-iorn casserole dish. Place the shank in the dish and roast for about 45 minutes until the skin begins to crisp and the fat renders in the bottom of the dish. Turn the shank every 15 minutes to ensure even cooking. Temporarily remove the dish from the oven and transfer the shank to a plate.

Pound the garlic, ginger and white pepper to a paste in a pestle and mortar, using the coarse sea salt as an abrasive.

Place the dish from the oven over a medium heat and fry the paste in the oil, stirring constantly until it is golden brown. Then add the stock, fish sauce, palm sugar, sweet soy sauce, cassia bark, bay leaves and oyster sauce. Add the pork shank back to the dish, making sure it is submerged in the stock; add a little more stock if necessary. Cover with a lid and return to the oven for about 3 hours. After this time, the meat should fall off the bone and the sauce should be loose but rich in taste, almost like a broth. Add the eggs in their shells and soft-boil them in the sauce for 5 minutes, then remove and peel the shell.

Serve the pork shredded off the bone in bowls, with the noodles underneath and one egg cut in half per bowl. Pour over the hot broth and serve sprinkled with the coriander. This dish is also delicious served with steamed jasmine rice, if you prefer.

WARM COCONUT, TURMERIC, GARLIC AND TIGER PRAWN VERMICELLI NOODLE SALAD

10g fresh red turmeric, peeled (or 1 tablespoon dried turmeric)

6 garlic cloves, peeled

2 red bird's-eye chillies

3cm piece of ginger, peeled and roughly chopped

1 tablespoon chopped coriander roots (optional)

1 teaspoon coarse sea salt

2 tablespoons vegetable oil

6 fresh tiger prawns, deveined

1 tablespoon fish sauce

1 teaspoon caster sugar

200ml coconut cream

150g fine vermicelli rice noodles, blanched for 1 minute in boiling salted water and then refreshed in cold water

2 spring onions, finely shredded

20g Thai shallots, peeled and sliced (or any sweet shallot)

10g mint leaves, slightly torn

10g coriander, chopped

10g chives, roughly chopped

1 lime, cut into wedges, to serve

sweet chilli sauce (see page 150), to serve

This was a dish I created when I was cooking in the markets in London throughout the summer. If there are two things you can be sure people are going to want to eat in the sunshine, it's prawns and noodles. This recipe combines the two and was always a hit. To make it a little more special, use a few king prawns. Although much more expensive, they are ideal for munching with lots of noodles and curry sauce. Just make sure you serve this with lots of napkins or you'll be cleaning up the turmeric stains for months.

Pound the turmeric, garlic, chillies, ginger and coriander roots to a coarse paste in a pestle and mortar, using the salt as an abrasive.

In a large frying pan or wok, heat the oil on a medium–high heat and fry the paste, stirring constantly to avoid it sticking to the pan. When the paste begins to turn golden brown, add the prawns and fry for a further 2–3 minutes until they are pink and cooked through. Add the fish sauce and sugar, and fry for a further 30 seconds to caramelise the sugar; the paste will begin to darken at this stage. Add the coconut cream, blanched noodles, spring onions, shallots, mint, coriander and chives, and delicately toss everything together in the pan, allowing the noodles, salad and prawns to mix and be coated in the sauce.

Serve in bowls with wedges of lime. This salad is also great served with a good helping of sweet chilli sauce.

100ml vegetable oil

100g red curry paste

4 tablespoons fish sauce

2 whole sea bass, descaled, cleaned and gutted, bloodline and gills removed, scoured down to the bone

2 litres sunflower oil

8 garlic cloves, peeled and bashed, to garnish

10 dried long red chillies, to garnish

6 kaffir lime leaves, stems removed, to garnish

10g Thai sweet basil, to garnish

sticky rice, to serve

smoky chilli oil (see page 155), to serve

sweet fish sauce (*nam prik nam pla*) (see page 151), to serve

DRY RED CURRY OF FRIED SEA BASS, CHILLI AND CRISPY LIME LEAVES AND BASIL

Visually this dish is quite amazing, but it is not one for the squeamish. It involves deep-frying the whole fish and having diners pick through it themselves. The red curry paste is rubbed into the fish before it is deep-fried, creating almost a dry red curry dish. If you like, this can be topped with more red curry, cooked with some coconut cream. However, I like to eat this one dry, with some sticky glutinous rice and some dipping sauces (see pages 151 and 155).

Start by marinating the fish. In a bowl, mix the vegetable oil, red curry paste and fish sauce. Then using both hands, rub the paste into the skin until the fish is thoroughly coated and leave to marinate for 30 minutes.

Heat the sunflower oil in a large, deep saucepan to about 160°C; this temperature is high enough to fry the fish without drying it out.

Fry the garnishes first. Have a tray lined with kitchen paper to the ready, then fry the garlic. Check that the oil is not too hot by dropping in a small piece of garlic – if it bubbles gently and floats to the top, the temperature is just right and the garlic will turn golden brown in about 2 minutes. Use a slotted spoon to transfer the garlic onto kitchen paper. Spread the fried garlic out using a fork to ensure the oil rolls off it. Repeat with the dried chillies, kaffir lime leaves and basil, but bear in mind they cook in about 30 seconds.

Next, fry the fish in the oil. Using two tongs, place the fish in a horseshoe shape in the oil; when it cooks in this shape it is possible for the fish to stand up on the plate. Fry the fish for 4–5 minutes; the skin should be crispy and the meat juicy. Remove from the pan and set aside to rest for a few minutes.

Serve the fish stacked up on a plate, topped with all the garnishes and accompanied by sticky rice and dipping sauces: smoky chilli oil and *nam prik nam pla* are my favourites.

SMOKED SALMON AND CRAB CRISPY VERMICELLI NOODLE SALAD

300ml vegetable oil

50g fine vermicelli rice noodles

50g banana shallots, peeled and thinly sliced

80g yellow bean sauce

50g caster sugar

30ml pickled garlic juice (or distilled white vinegar)

4 eggs, cracked into a bowl

30ml lime juice

50ml clementine juice (or mandarins)

50g brown crab meat

10g Chinese chives, finely chopped (or regular chives)

15g beansprouts

2 long red chillies, julienned

4 kaffir lime leaves, julienned

1 head of pickled garlic, thinly sliced

150g smoked salmon fillet, flaked into bite-sized pieces

10g coriander, chopped

1 mandarin, cut into wedges, to serve

1 lime, cut into wedges, to serve

This is known as *mi krob* in Thailand, which pretty much means 'crisp noodles'. It's an explosion of flavour all held together by a rich sweet, salty and sour yellow bean sauce. Traditionally, they use a citrus fruit called a *som saa* to add a kick to this salad, but this version uses clementines, which are more readily available. I like to smoke my own salmon as I have a barbecue with a lid. If you also have one, lightly coat a side of salmon in melted butter and hot smoke for 20 minutes; if not, shop bought is absolutely fine.

In a large saucepan, heat 250ml of the vegetable oil to about 190°C until it is smoking hot; the noodles need this heat to pop. Have a tray lined with kitchen paper at the ready, then fry the noodles in small bundles. As they cook they will burst into a size roughly three times their size. When this happens, take them straight out and drain on kitchen paper. The noodles will turn from translucent to white; try not to let them turn golden brown as there is a fine line between brown and black with these noodles.

Heat the remaining oil in a large wok on a high heat and add the shallots, stirring all the time so that they cook evenly. There is a little more oil than you would normally use because the shallots are essentially being shallow-fried. When they begin to turn golden brown, add the yellow bean sauce and continue to scrape and stir until the paste begins to darken. Reduce the heat, add the sugar and cook for about 1 minute; the paste will darken quickly so be careful. Add the pickled garlic juice and turn off the heat. Now we're going to temper the eggs into this: slowly add the hot yellow bean mixture into the eggs while constantly whisking. The slower you do this the more chance of success. The heat from the sauce will slowly cook the eggs without scrambling them and the sauce will thicken and turn glossy. Return the mixture to a low heat, then add the lime and clementine juices and the crab meat and whisk thoroughly. Taste the sauce: it should be sweet, salty and sour.

To finish the salad, add the chives, beansprouts, chillies, lime leaves, garlic, salmon and coriander to a large mixing bowl and combine well. Pour the warm dressing over the top and serve, garnished with wedges of mandarin and lime.

SLOW-BRAISED BEEF SHORT RIB _{WITH} A SCOTCH BONNET DIPPING SAUCE

SERVES 4
(WITH A LITTLE EXTRA SAUCE –
WHY NOT!)

GF
OPTIONAL

150ml vegetable oil

3 sticks lemongrass

15 Thai shallots, peeled and left whole (or other shallots)

2 pandan leaves, tied in a knot

6 kaffir lime leaves, torn

4 beef short rib, on the bone

500ml hot beef stock

500ml coconut cream

150ml fish sauce

2 tablespoons table salt

3 heads of garlic, sliced in half across the cloves

200g scotch bonnets, stems and seeds removed from 100g

50g palm sugar

50ml distilled white vinegar

50ml oyster sauce (optional)

10g coriander, chopped, to serve

steamed jasmine rice, to serve

This is another of my own creations. One of my favourite things when eating Thai food is the endless array of different chilli jams, relishes and dipping sauces. So at Farang we wanted to make a sauce that blew your mind – a sauce to end all sauces. This is it. Using roasted scotch bonnets sweetens the chillies, making them much kinder on the palette and the inclusion of roasted garlic also helps to soften things. However, be aware that this is still a pokey sauce. Serve with rice and a sharp salad to combat the heat. And wear gloves to remove the seeds from the scotch bonnets!

Preheat the oven to 120°C/gas mark ½. Heat 50ml of the oil in a large ovenproof casserole dish, then add the lemongrass, Thai shallots, pandan and kaffir lime leaves, and toss everything in the hot oil to release the flavours. Add the short rib and quickly sear the meat on all sides, then submerge the beef in the stock and coconut cream, 100ml of the fish sauce and the salt. Cover with a lid and transfer to the oven for 6 hours. This slow cooking allows the collagen in the meat to break down slowly so that the meat is tender and soft. The meat is ready when it can be cut with a spoon and almost falls off the rib.

Meanwhile, put the remaining oil in an ovenproof pan and place the garlic, cut-side down, in the oil along with the chillies. Roast for 25–30 minutes, until the garlic has softened and the chillies are blistered and soft and everything smells fragrant. Remove from the oven and allow to cool, then squeeze the garlic out and discard the skins (keep the oil for later use). Place the roasted garlic and chillies in a food processor along with with the palm sugar, vinegar, oyster sauce, the remaining fish sauce and 50ml of the roasted garlic/chilli oil and blend to a sauce. It should taste sweet, salty, sour, smoky and very hot. If it is too hot for you, add some coconut cream to ease the heat a little.

Serve the ribs with steamed jasmine rice, heaps of sauce for dipping and scattered with coriander.

ROAST SATAY CHICKEN
with CHINESE CHIVES
and LIME

SERVES 4   GF

4 tablespoons vegetable oil

200g peanut satay
curry paste (see page 160)

2 tablespoons palm sugar

2 tablespoons fish sauce

100ml hot chicken stock

2 tablespoons tamarind paste
(optional)

200ml coconut cream

1 whole chicken,
spatchcocked

steamed jasmine rice,
to serve

10g Chinese chives, chopped
(or regular chives), to serve

1 lime, cut into wedges,
to serve

4 tablespoons roasted
peanuts, lightly crushed,
to garnish

4 tablespoons pickled ginger
(optional), to garnish

This dish can very easily replace a traditional roast dinner. By marinating the chicken overnight, the salt and sugar in the curry paste act like a brine, as well as a marinade, resulting in an amazingly flavoursome, tender chicken that then just needs to be thrown in the oven. The creamy, peanut sauce benefits greatly from some crunchy fresh chives and a squeeze of fresh lime – add a few teaspoons of smoked chilli powder, too, if you like things hot!

In a large non-stick frying pan, heat the oil over a high heat. Add the curry paste and fry for 10–12 minutes, stirring and scraping until it darkens slightly and smells fragrant. Add the palm sugar, reduce the heat to medium, and continue to stir and scrape until the sugar caramelises and the paste darkens further. Add the fish sauce, which will deglaze any paste that has stuck to the pan, then remove the pan from the heat, add the stock, tamarind paste and coconut cream, and mix well. Allow to cool.

Place the chicken in a roasting tray and coat it all over with the cooked-out curry paste. Leave to marinate for a minimum of 2 hours, but ideally overnight in the refrigerator.

Preheat the oven to 200°C/gas mark 6. Roast the chicken for 40–45 minutes. The paste should begin to crisp a little and the chicken juices should run into the curry paste. Check that the chicken is cooked through by making an incision in the leg all the way to the bone to check for signs of blood. If the juices do not run clear, return the chicken to the oven for a further 5–10 minutes. For best results, use a temperature probe; since the chicken has essentially been brined, you can take it out at 70°C and it will still be moist. Allow to rest for 5 minutes before serving.

Serve the chicken with steamed jasmine rice and sprinkle with the chives. Serve with wedges of lime and top with the peanuts and pickled ginger (if using).

CURRIED EGG NOODLES WITH BBQ BUTTERNUT SQUASH

By Dan Turner
Sous chef at Farang

2 medium butternut squashes, peeled and cut into chunks

4 long red chillies

5 garlic bulbs

10 medium round shallots

6 stalks of lemongrass

2.5cm piece of galangal

2 pieces of fresh red turmeric

1 tablespoon coriander seeds

seeds from 1 black cardamom pod

4 coriander roots, finely sliced

a pinch of coarse sea salt

75ml coconut oil

2 tablespoons fish sauce

1 tablespoon mild curry powder

2 tablespoons dark soy sauce

2 tablespoons palm sugar

150ml chicken or vegetable stock

500ml coconut cream

400g flat egg noodles, blanched in salted water and drained

2 litres vegetable oil, for deep-frying

a handful of chopped coriander, to garnish

3 Thai shallots, sliced, to garnish

roasted chilli oil, to serve

1 lime, cut into wedges, to serve

This recipe is really just a guide and experienced cooks can play around with the quantities and cooking methods.

Blanch the squash in salted water for 6–8 minutes until soft on the outside but still reasonably firm. Drain and allow to cool briefly before smearing with a little oil. Place on a hot barbecue and cover. Check after a 4–5 minutes and turn once they start to char. They will be cooked once soft in the middle. Next, scorch the chillies over the coals until slightly blackened, then set aside. Place the garlic and shallots on the grill and turn when the outsides start to blacken, remove when soft to the touch – but be careful not to burn your fingers. Grill the lemongrass, galangal and turmeric until coloured but not black.

Take a pan, place on a low heat and gently toast the coriander seeds until fragrant. Do the same with the black cardamom seeds. Grind the spices to a fine powder in a pestle and mortar.

Slice off the top and bottom parts of the lemongrass, remove the outer sheath and finely slice. Peel the galangal, removing any stalk and finely chop. Cut off the bottom of the garlic bulb and squeeze out the flesh. Peel and chop the shallots, roughly chop the chillies and peel the turmeric. In a pestle and mortar, pound the coriander roots to a paste. Add the lemongrass and continue to pound, then add the galangal, turmeric, chillies, shallots and garlic in that order, making sure a smooth paste is achieved before adding the next ingredient. Finally, stir in the pounded spices.

Heat the coconut oil in a large pan on a medium high heat. Add the curry paste and cook for 6–8 minutes, scraping the base of the pan so it doesn't burn, then add the fish sauce, curry powder, soy sauce and sugar. Reduce the heat so the sugar melts and caramelises, then stir in the stock and coconut cream and simmer for 8–10 minutes.

Meanwhile, fill a pan with the oil to deep-fry some of the noodles and heat to 190°C. Using a large slotted spoon, or pair of tongs, place a small handful of noodles in the hot oil. It will spit and splutter so stand back. Fry for 40–50 seconds, then turn them over and fry for a further 30 seconds or so until golden. Remove and place on kitchen towel to drain.

Place the remaining noodles and butternut squash in the simmering curry and heat through. The curry should not be too thick, but almost like a soup, and have a thin coconut oil slick on top. Serve in large, deep bowls, garnished with coriander, a few sliced Thai shallots and your deep-fried noodles. Drizzle over a little roasted chilli oil. It should taste smoky, rich, salty and sweet with a spicy edge. Squeeze a wedge of lime over to add a sour element.

STEAMED PORK RIBS
WITH ROASTED RICE, THAI AUBERGINES AND BASIL

By Deirdre Kane
Director at Cooking Happy Thai Cookery School

This is a variation of a north-eastern Thai dish that is quick to get together once you have all the ingredients to hand. It's a great one to cook for the family, as it can be prepared ahead. It is also impressive and gets a lot of admiration. I teach it in my Thai cooking classes and I love seeing people's faces as they open their parcels. Chicken pieces also work well; you don't need to pre-cook them (though make sure they are small), just cook them out in the paste before wrapping in the banana leaf. When pounding the paste, you start with the hardest and driest ingredients first, followed by the softest and wettest. Gapi (shrimp paste) is optional. I find that people who regularly eat Thai food enjoy the taste of the gapi more, in other words it's a flavour you may need to grow to love.

Place the pork ribs in steamer set over a pan of simmering water and steam for 20 minutes. Set aside and reserve the liquid.

Soak the chillies in warm, salted water for 30 minutes, then drain.

Make the paste by pounding the ingredients in the order listed, making sure each ingredient has been reduced to a paste before adding the next.

Heat the coconut oil in a medium saucepan and cook the the paste until fragrant, about 10 minutes. Add the palm sugar and cook until it has become a dark rich colour. Season with the fish sauce .

Add the ribs to the saucepan, plus some of the cooking liquor to make a semi loose curry. Simmer for a further 2–3 minutes, then check the seasoning, it should be balanced, salty and hot. Stir in the rest of the ingredients and heat through.

Lay the banana leaf strips one on top of each other, shiny side down. Place a quarter of the mixture in the middle of these leaves and then bring the edges together two at a time. At the same time lift opposing edges towards each other and then using tooth picks, weave them together, almost as if you are wrapping a Christmas present and the banana leaves are the wrapping paper and the toothpicks the tape. Then repeat this process with the other two sides, securing the mixture within the folded parcel, repeat this with the rest of the mixture and banana leaves.

Steam for 20 minutes and allow to cool slightly before opening.

1 rack of pork ribs, cut into single ribs

100g coconut oil

1 tablespoon palm sugar

3 tablespoons fish sauce

2 apple aubergines, quartered

50g pea aubergines

2 tablespoons roasted ground rice (see tip below)

2g Thai basil shredded

3 banana leaves, cut into 4 x 40cm strips, rubbed with a little oil to give a shine

FOR THE PASTE

100g long red chillies, deseeded

a large pinch of sea salt

3 small red or green chillies

100g galangal

250g lemongrass

2 tablespoons chopped coriander roots

100g Thai shallots

½ tablespoon gapi (shrimp paste), optional

TIPS

Roasted rice powder is used in salads and dipping sauces to add depth of flavour and texture. To make, toast a couple of teaspoons of glutinous rice in a dry frying pan over a medium heat for 8-10 minutes, moving constantly until golden brown and fragrant. Immediately grind this to a fine powder using a pestle and mortar.

CURRIES AND BIG ONES

2 x 10cm sticks of cassia bark
(or cinamon)

6 star anise

10 cloves

1 teaspoon coriander seeds

1 teaspoon fennel seeds

20 whole white peppercorns

5cm piece peeled ginger

5 coriander roots

5 garlic cloves

1.5kg good quality pork belly,
cut into 5cm chunks

2 tablespoons table salt

1.5 litres chicken stock

110g palm sugar

100ml fish sauce

3 tablespoons oyster sauce

2 tablespoons dark soy sauce
or dark sweet soy sauce
(kecap manis)

1 piece of mandarin peel

2½cm piece of galangal,
bruised (optional)

2 pandan leaves, knotted
(optional)

300g block of firm tofu, and
enough plain oil to deep-fry it

6 soft boiled eggs

coriander leaves, chopped,
to garnish

PORK BELLY BRAISED IN 5 SPICE BROTH WITH SOFT COOKED EGG AND FRIED TOFU

By Andy Oliver
Head chef and co-founder Som Saa, London

This is my version of the classic Thai-Chinese dish _mu parlow_. It keeps really well and perhaps even tastes better the next day. It's delicious with Sebby's burnt chilli sauce (see page 146).

First make the spice powder. Dry-fry the spices over a medium heat, until fragrant and toasted, then allow to cool. Now hold back one toasted stick of cassia bark and 2 star anise, transfer the rest to a spice grinder and grind to a fine powder.

Next make the paste. Pound the white peppercorns in a pestle and mortar into a rough powder, then add the ginger, coriander roots and garlic and pound into a coarse paste. Set aside.

Add the pork belly chunks to a large pan and cover with cold water. Place on a high heat, and add the salt. When the pot boils, drain the pork (discarding the liquid) and wash under cold water. Set aside for later.

Place a heavy-based pan on a medium heat, add the oil and, when hot, add the paste and fry until light golden and fragrant. Add the spice powder and fry for 30 more seconds, then add the chicken stock, sugar, fish sauce, oyster sauce and kecap manis and bring to the boil.

Add the blanched pork and reserved whole cinnamon stick and star anise, mandarin peel and (if using) the galangal and pandan leaves too. Reduce the heat to a gentle simmer and cook the pork very slowly on the stove for about 1½ hours or until the pork is tender but the pieces are still holding together.

While the pork is braising, cut the tofu into 2½cm cubes and deep-fry in the oil until golden. Set aside.

When the braise is ready, turn off the heat allow to cool for 5 minutes, then add the tofu and soft eggs. Leave them to marinate in the warm sauce for at least 15 minutes, ideally an hour. Serve with jasmine rice.

5 DIPS, PICKLES & PASTES

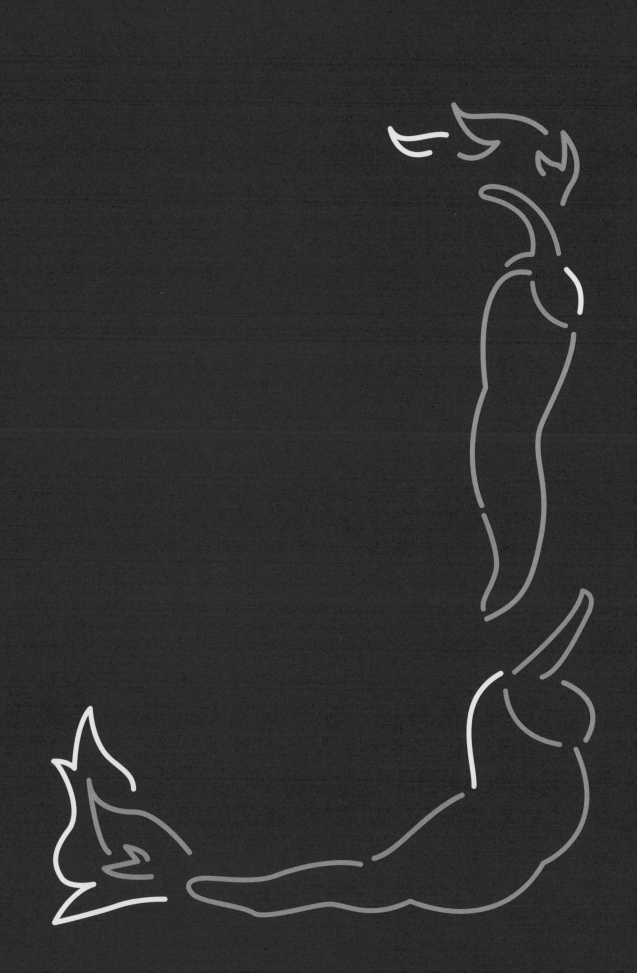

MAKES
ABOUT 800ML
(10–15 SERVINGS, DEPENDING
ON HOW GREEDY YOU ARE)

1 litre vegetable oil

1 large head of garlic,
peeled and minced

500g long red chillies,
pricked with a fork

100ml fish sauce
(or soy sauce)

50ml oyster sauce (optional)

50ml distilled white vinegar

50g palm sugar (or soft dark
brown sugar)

coriander leaves, chopped,
to garnish

BURNT CHILLI DIPPING SAUCE WITH CRISPY GARLIC

The ketchup of the Thai world, but better! This is one of those sauces that will make you wonder where the bloody hell you've been all your life. It's perfect with pork belly, or as an addition to soups to add depth of flavour. To be honest, though, I've seen chefs eat it with absolutely everything – salads, stews, sauces, even as a dip with crisps (you know who you are!), so go nuts.

Heat the oil in a large saucepan until it reaches 180°C. A tell-tale sign that it's ready is when you can see a slight movement in the oil. Have to hand a tray lined with kitchen paper, plus a sieve placed on top of another pan that is deep enough to contain the used oil.

Check the oil is hot enough by dropping in a little garlic and seeing how it reacts; it should fizz lots but then settle quickly to a gentle bubble. If it makes a loud noise, the oil is too hot. When ready, add all the garlic and stir carefully with a long-handled spoon to separate any clumps. Fry for about 1 minute until the garlic begins to turn golden brown, then very carefully pour the oil through the sieve and set aside. Tip the garlic from the sieve onto the kitchen paper; it will crisp up as the oil drains and cools.

Char the chillies under a hot grill, but keep an eye on them as if they're black all over they will end up being very bitter. Allow to cool slightly, remove the stems and blitz in a food processor straight away – the residual heat from the still-warm chillies makes the sauce come together better.

Add the remaining ingredients, plus 6 tablespoons of the garlic oil, to a food processor and blitz until combined; the sauce should be a light red–orange colour and taste sweet, sour and hot. At this point, the mixture can be stored in a sterilised jar in the fridge indefinitely. If you are serving immediately, top with the crispy garlic and some coriander leaves.

MAKES
ABOUT 200ML
(2-3 SERVINGS)

4 Thai purple aubergines
(or regular aubergines)

juice of I lime

I teaspoon chilli powder

juice of ½ clementine

2 tablespoons fish sauce
(or soy sauce)

I teaspoon caster sugar
(or light soft brown sugar)

I teaspoon thick
tamarind water

10g coriander, chopped

I tablespoon chopped
coriander roots

GRILLED
AUBERGINE RELISH

This wonderful creation fuses the intense smokiness of grilled aubergine with the freshness of lime and an underlying kick of smoked chilli. It is best eaten with rare beef, as a dipping sauce, but is delicious at the side of any grilled meat or fish.

Light the barbecue and, using a pair of tongs, place the aubergines directly onto the hot coals, or near the hottest part of the grill if you're using a gas barbecue. Keep a close eye on them and turn them over frequently, ensuring that the heat from the coals is distributed evenly. The aubergines are ready when they are soft to the touch, with charred and blistering skins. Place to one side until cool enough to handle then peel the skin off so you are left with the smoky, meaty goodness within. If you are not using a barbecue, crank the oven right up to full blast and bake the aubergines until the skins are charred and the flesh is soft – this will take 20–25 minutes.

Put the aubergines and all the other ingredients in a pestle and mortar or food processor. Combine to a coarse paste and serve immediately. The relish can be kept in the fridge for 2–3 days, but will need re-seasoning as the flavours are likely to go flat.

MAKES
ABOUT 500G
(10-12 SERVINGS)

20ml fish sauce (or soy sauce)

I teaspoon table salt

3 kaffir lime leaves, torn

200ml distilled white vinegar

200g caster sugar

250g Thai shallots, peeled
(or any small, sweet shallots)

250g cashew nuts, roasted

50g ginger, peeled and sliced
wafer thin

I lime (if serving immediately)

PICKLED THAI SHALLOTS,
CASHEWS AND GINGER

This pickle is delicious served with curries, salads and roti. It also keeps almost indefinitely in the fridge, so I like to make it in bulk so it is ready to pull out and serve alongside pretty much everything.

In a medium saucepan, bring the fish sauce, salt, kaffir lime leaves, vinegar, sugar and 200ml water to a simmer, stirring until the sugar and salt have dissolved. Turn off the heat and add the remaining ingredients – the shallots and cashews will soften slightly from the heat of the liquor without cooking through completely to offer a lovely textural crunch. Allow the pickles to cool, then store in a sterilised jar in the fridge. When serving, freshen up with a little squeeze of lime juice.

MAKES
ABOUT 1 LITRE

2 tablespoons roughly
chopped coriander roots

500g long red chillies,
stems removed and
roughly chopped

100g green bird's-eye chillies,
stems removed and roughly
chopped

3 heads of garlic, peeled

1 teaspoon coarse sea salt

1 litre white vinegar

1kg caster sugar

2 tablespoons fish sauce
(or soy sauce)

1 teaspoon table salt

1 stick lemongrass, bruised

5 whole limes, juiced but
keep the skins

FIERY SWEET CHILLI
AND FRESH LIME

**If you ever walk into my house and can't find sweet chilli
in the fridge, then you'd better start worrying, because
something serious must have gone down. It's the perfect
condiment for most fried snacks and, as you'll see, I've
offered a few recipes in this book that are delicious eaten
with this sauce at their side. It can be kept in the fridge
indefinitely but you may want to add a fresh squeeze of
lime after a week or so to freshen it up.**

Pound the coriander roots, red and green chillies, and garlic to a chunky
paste in a pestle and mortar or food processor, using the coarse sea salt as
an abrasive.

In a large, deep saucepan, heat the vinegar, sugar, fish sauce, table salt,
lemongrass and lime skins on a medium heat until the sugar has dissolved.
Add the paste and stir well, then bring to the boil and simmer for
45–50 minutes until the sugar has caramelised and the sauce is thick; it
helps to leave a large metal spoon resting against the side of the pan as
this stops the mixture from bubbling over. To check whether it is ready,
place a teaspoon of the mixture onto a cold plate and leave for 1 minute
to cool, then tilt the plate downwards. Look at the way the sweet chilli
runs down the plate – it should be thick and slowly trickle down the plate,
rather than pour straight off it. If it is still too thin, return it to the heat
and test again every 10 minutes.

When you are happy that the mixture is thick enough, remove
the pan from the heat and leave to cool, then discard the lime skins and
lemongrass, and stir in the lime juice. Stored in a sterilised jar, this can be
kept in the fridge for up to two months. However, it will benefit from a
fresh squirt of lime juice after it's been in the fridge for over a week to
freshen it up.

SWEET FISH SAUCE

MAKES ABOUT 350ML (3-4 SERVINGS)

GF

VE OPTIONAL

Known as *nam prik nam pla*, this is a very popular Thai condiment, usually left on the table for diners to help themselves to, in the same way that salt and pepper is here. I can near enough drink fish sauce these days, so for me it's a necessary addition to many meals. Traditionally, it just includes garlic, chillies and lime juice, but I like to sweeten it up a little and also add the skin of the limes and clementines for a little bitterness.

Simply mix all the ingredients together in a bowl and serve. This sauce will keep for 3–4 days in the fridge, but the herbs will go brown quite quickly, so it is best eaten straight away.

300ml fish sauce (or soy sauce)

1 lime (½ juiced and ½ diced)

1 clementine (½ juiced and ½ diced)

2 red bird's-eye chillies, chopped

2 green bird's-eye chillies, chopped

1 teaspoon caster sugar

10g coriander leaves, chopped

2 garlic cloves, peeled and thinly sliced

15g ginger, peeled and thinly sliced

ROASTED CHILLI RELISH 'NAM JIM JAEW'

MAKES ABOUT 400G (5-6 SERVINGS)

GF

VE OPTIONAL

Threading the ingredients onto skewers means they can be barbecued with ease. They will soften and char at different rates, because of their moisture content and size. Leave the skins on where possible, as this will help them to smoke and roast within. *Nam jim jaew,* translated from Thai essentially means 'excellent dipping sauce', a fitting name for this lovely condiment.

Light the barbecue to a high heat. I much prefer to cook this over wood, although, charcoal or even gas will work fine. Grill each vegetable skewer, turning regularly to ensure that the vegetables are softened and lightly charred around the outside.

Remove the skewers from the heat and set aside until cool enough to handle. Remove the chilli stems and the garlic and shallot skins. Remove the core and the tough outer sheaths of the lemongrass, then chop the soft part of the lemongrass into small pieces. Add all this to a food processor or large pestle and mortar with the tamarind water, palm sugar, fish sauce, chilli powder and coriander roots, and pound or blitz to a moist, coarse paste. Finally, stir in the lime juice and check for seasoning: the relish should be smoky, spicy, salty and sour.

50g tomatoes, skewered

6 long red chillies, skewered

6 green bird's-eye chillies, skewered

10 garlic cloves, skewered

50g Thai shallots (or any small shallots), skewered

4 banana shallots, skewered

2 sticks lemongrass, bruised

2 tablespoons thick tamarind water

2 tablespoons palm sugar (or soft light brown sugar)

2 tablespoons fish sauce (or soy sauce)

2 teaspoons smoked chilli powder

2 tablespoons chopped coriander roots

juice of 2 limes

MAKES 800G
(12-15 SERVINGS)

ROASTED TOMATO PICKLE

400g cherry tomatoes

4 beef tomatoes, each sliced
into 8 chunks

400g green tomatoes

200g long red chillies

100g long green chillies

2 heads of garlic, broken
into cloves but not peeled

6 banana shallots

30ml olive oil

2 whole limes (1 juiced and
1 diced with the zest still on)

3 tablespoons soy sauce
(or fish sauce)

2 tablespoons distilled
white vinegar

3 tablespoons tamarind

2 tablespoons chopped
coriander roots

2 tablespoons palm sugar
(or soft dark brown sugar)

½ teaspoon table salt

**I've given large quantities here as the uses for this relish are
pretty much universal; it works well as a dipping sauce for
grilled meats and fish and is also delicious tossed through
a stir-fry or salad.**

Preheat the oven to 180°C/gas mark 4. Place all the vegetables in
a roasting tray and drizzle with the olive oil. Roast each vegetable until
slightly charred and soft within. The time this takes will differ for each
vegetable, so check every 15 minutes and remove each ingredient as
it is ready.

Peel the garlic and shallots and discard any tomato vines and chilli
stalks. Pound all the vegetables in a pestle and mortar (or a food processor,
although I prefer the pickle to be chunky) together with the diced limes,
lime juice, soy sauce, vinegar, tamarind, coriander roots, palm sugar and salt.

The pickle should taste smoky, sour, spicy and savoury, with a hint of
bitterness from the lime zest. It will keep in the fridge for a few weeks, but
will need re-seasoning with a little lime juice as the flavours will go flat.
If you want to store this for longer, place the mixture into sterilised jars.

GRILLED CHILLI, GARLIC
AND LIME DIPPING SAUCE

2 tablespoons chopped
coriander roots

8 garlic cloves, peeled

8 long green chillies, roasted
in the oven at 180°C/gas
mark 4 for 20 minutes, or
charred and softened on
the barbecue

a pinch of coarse sea salt

2 tablespoons caster sugar

juice of 4 limes

juice of 2 mandarins
(or clementines)

4 tablespoons fish sauce
(or soy sauce)

**This is amazing used as a dressing for seafood salads, as a
dipping sauce, as *nam jim* for grilled meats and fish, or poured
over rice for freshness and heat. It needs to be as fresh as
possible, to ensure the lime juice doesn't oxidise. Roasting
the chillies beforehand offers a more rounded, smoky finish,
but it isn't necessary and it can be made with bird's eye
chillies for a more intense chilli kick.**

Pound the coriander roots, garlic, then chillies (in that order) to a coarse
paste in a pestle and mortar, using the salt as an abrasive. Add the sugar
and pound for a few more seconds. You should aim for a relatively smooth
paste, though a little chunk is not the end of the world. Add the lime and
mandarin juices and the fish sauce. The sauce should taste sweet, salty,
sour and hot. Exact quantities are impossible to give as the strength of
the ingredients varies depending on where they are grown, so adjust the
seasoning to suit your tastes.

This dipping sauce can be kept in the fridge for 2–3 days, but will need
re-seasoning as the flavours are likely to go flat.

CHILLI VINEGAR

MAKES
ABOUT 200ML
(2-3 SERVINGS)

GF

VE
OPTIONAL

This is a must-have condiment that offers a sour and spicy burst to soups, noodles and stir fries. Known as *pik nam som*, it's often laid out on tables to give diners the chance to adjust their own seasoning.

Gently warm the vinegar in a saucepan with the salt and sugar until dissolved, then immediately remove the pan from the heat and set aside to cool. Add all the other ingredients, stir to combine and serve alongside lunch or dinner. Because of the lime juice, this will only keep for a few days in the fridge and is worth re-seasoning as the flavours may have gone flat.

100ml distilled white vinegar

½ teaspoon table salt

I teaspoon caster sugar

2 red bird's-eye chillies

2 green bird's-eye chillies

3 garlic cloves

I tablespoon fish sauce (or soy sauce)

juice of ½ lime

SMOKY CHILLI OIL

MAKES 550ML
(ABOUT 10 SERVINGS)

GF

VE
OPTIONAL

This is perfect as a dipping sauce, dressing or garnish and also drizzled into soups and curries for a little extra heat. It's very quick and easy to make and it lasts indefinitely sat out on the dinner table, so it's worth giving a go. The key is the chilli powder. Shop bought chilli powder can be used if you'd like (but it won't be as nice).

Toast 8–10 long red dried chillies in a dry wok until they char and begin to turn crispy and smoke. Remove them from the wok and allow to cool before crushing into a powder.

Combine all ingredients in a pestle and mortar or food processor until the sugar has dissolved. Taste for flavour: the oil should be sweet, salty, sour, rich and very spicy.

500ml olive oil

3 teaspoons chilli powder

2 tablespoons palm sugar

2 tablespoons fish sauce (or soy sauce)

2 tablespoons thick tamarind water

SPICY RED CHILLI
AND LIME SAUCE

2 tablespoons chopped
coriander roots

8 garlic cloves, peeled

4 long red chillies, stems
removed, deseeded and
roughly chopped

a pinch of coarse sea salt

2 tablespoons caster sugar

juice of 4 limes

juice of 2 mandarins
(or clementines)

4 tablespoons fish sauce
(or soy sauce)

Nam yum **is essentially the same as a** *nam jim,* **but as it uses
sweeter, less harsh red chillies it offers a slightly milder chilli
hit, making it ideal as a salad dressing. However, it can also
be made using red bird's eye chillies, in which case it's better
as a dipping sauce.**

Pound the coriander roots, garlic, then chillies (in that order) to a coarse
paste in a pestle and mortar, using the salt as an abrasive. Add the sugar
and pound for a few more seconds. You should aim for a relatively smooth
paste, though a little chunk is not the end of the world. Add the lime and
mandarin juices and the fish sauce. The sauce should taste sweet, salty,
sour and hot. Exact quantities are impossible to give, as the strength of
the ingredients varies depending on where they are grown, so adjust the
seasoning to suit your tastes.

This dipping sauce can be kept in the fridge for 2–3 days but as it is
likely to go flat the seasoning will need adjusting when you serve.

CHILLI PICKLED CUCUMBER AND LIME

MAKES 4 SERVINGS

GF

VE

100g palm sugar

100ml distilled white vinegar

juice of 2 limes

1 cucumber, chopped in half widthways, then peeled into thin strips using a vegetable peeler

2 long red chillies, deseeded and fine julienned

¼ teaspoon table salt

1 tablespoon smoked chilli powder (blue tongue)

This only takes minutes to throw together and works well tossed through salads, or eaten with curries. I use smoked chilli powder, which in the industry we call 'blue tongue', though I have no idea why? I guess it's something to do with the fact that it is bloody hot!

In a saucepan, gently melt the palm sugar in the vinegar and 100ml water, then remove the pan from the heat and allow to cool. Add all the other ingredients, stir, then and refrigerate until ready to serve. For the best results, eat immediately or within 2–3 days.

MAKES ABOUT 1KG
(5-6 SERVINGS)

PEANUT SATAY CURRY PASTE

80g large dried red chilies, cut in half, soaked in warm water to soften, then drained and deseeded

100g coriander roots, finely chopped

250g banana shallots, peeled and finely chopped

250g garlic, peeled

250g ginger, peeled and finely chopped

250g desiccated coconut

150g roasted peanuts

a large pinch of coarse salt

The success of this relies on a granite pestle and mortar. When making any curry paste, the objective is to combine flavours with brute force and a heavy weighted pestle and mortar is the fastest way to victory. Trust me, I first bought a wooden one for use at home and spent entire evenings bashing coriander root until my hands hurt and I swear it just got bigger. Using a food processor is not ideal as it chops the ingredients rather than mashing them into a paste. If you must use one, I recommend giving the blade as much help as possible by finely chopping all ingredients beforehand.

This paste is incredibly versatile and can be used for meat, fish and vegetables in a range of different ways. Traditionally, it is cooked out in coconut oil and let out with coconut cream and stock and seasoned with palm sugar, tamarind and fish or soy sauce. It's great both as a curry and as a dipping sauce.

In a large mortar, pound all the ingredients one at a time until each forms a smooth paste. Transfer each individual paste into a bowl before pounding the next ingredient.

When all the ingredients have had a good bashing, place them all together in the mortar again and pound to a smooth paste. This process will take quite some time but is worth it! Transfer to an airtight container and keep refrigerated. Because of the coconut content, this paste will only keep for about a week.

CRISPY CHILLI AND COCONUT JAM

MAKES
ABOUT 500ML
(8–10 SERVINGS, DEPENDING
ON HOW GREEDY YOU ARE)

GF

1 litre vegetable oil

100g banana shallots, peeled and thinly sliced

100g garlic cloves, peeled and thinly sliced

3cm piece of ginger, peeled and thinly sliced

20g dried prawns (optional)

50g dried long red chillies

75g palm sugar, roughly chopped (or soft dark brown sugar)

50ml fish sauce (add an extra 50ml if not using dried prawns)

50ml tamarind water

a little coconut cream, if serving immediately as a dip

The key to this jam lies in the consistency of the deep-fried ingredients. Each one needs to be sliced wafer thin – either using a very sharp knife or a mandolin – so they cook at an even rate and you get a light golden crisp. This can be a difficult game to get right as each stage takes a long time and has the potential to go epically wrong at any moment if the oil gets too hot – the last thing that you want to do is to burn your wafer-thin slivers (or your hands!).

However, although this jam takes a little effort, you will certainly be pleased to have it in the kitchen. It's great served as a dip and as a relish and salad dressing. Also, the palm sugar and oil act as a preservative, giving it an incredibly a long shelf life – it can be kept in the fridge almost indefinitely.

Pour the oil into a large wok and heat until it reaches 200°C. To test that it is hot enough, drop in a few shallot slices; if they rise to the surface and bubble gently the oil is ready.

Start by frying the shallots as these have the highest moisture content and will take longer to fry. Gently drop them into the oil and, using a long-handled fork, stir to ensure they cook evenly. When golden brown, after 6–8 minutes, remove them with a slotted spoon and drain on kitchen paper. Pick the slices apart using two forks so none are stuck together. Repeat with the garlic, ginger, dried prawns and chillies (in that order).

Place all the deep-fried ingredients into a food processor, together with half the oil that was used for cooking (though be sure to let it cool first), and blitz until combined. Pour this into a saucepan, place on a low heat and add the palm sugar and fish sauce. Stir to dissolve the sugar and keep stirring until it caramelises, so that the jam thickens and clumps together. Remove from the heat, add the tamarind water, stir to combine and taste. The mixture should be sweet, salty, sour and hot – the magic is in the balance.

Before serving the jam, gently warm it in a pan and add a little coconut cream to loosen it.

MASSAMAN CURRY PASTE

10–12 sticks lemongrass, cut into small chunks

80g galangal, cut into small chunks

80g smoked dried red chillies, dry-fried until charred and crispy, then soaked in warm water for 30 minutes with as many seeds removed as possible

200g garlic

200g banana shallots

20g coriander roots

80g roasted peanuts

5g coarse sea salt

1 teaspoon Thai cardamom, husks removed, or ½ teaspoon Indian cardamom

40g coriander seeds

1 whole nutmeg, grated or chopped

1 teaspoon cloves

10g cassia bark (or 1 cinnamon stick)

2 sheathes of mace, snapped up small

20g cumin seeds

5g white peppercorns

Massaman is a truly remarkable curry – mild, aromatic, sweet and savoury, but with slightly mysterious origins. Some believe it comes from the central region of Thailand, others that it first popped up in the southern area of the country. However, the spices it uses indicate that its roots are in India, proving how excellently the Thais can take something and make it their own.

Most of the recipes I have been shown use dried red chillies that are first soaked and then pounded into the paste. I do exactly this, but first dry fry them in a pan so that they are smoking and beginning to char and then soak them. The change in flavour is massive; they offer a softer, more rounded heat after this process, perfect for this mild curry.

Pound the lemongrass, galangal, chillies, garlic, shallots, coriander and peanuts one at a time in a pestle and mortar until each forms a smooth paste, using the salt as an abrasive. Once all are pounded individually, combine them in the mortar to form one paste. Set aside.

Toast the spices in a frying pan. However, bear in mind that these all toast at different rates, so start with the cardamom, coriander seeds, then the nutmeg, cloves and cassia bark, shaking the pan constantly. As soon as the spices start to smoke a little, add the mace and cumin. Toast for another minute, then add the peppercorns and remove the pan from the heat and allow to cool a little.

Grind all the spices to a fine powder, then pound them into the paste. Keep mortaring and pestling away until you are left with a slightly moist, fairly smooth paste, with no identifiable chunks. However, bear in mind that massaman paste is dryer than most due to its heavy dry spice content.

Store the paste in an airtight container with some clingfilm over the paste to act as a barrier against oxidisation. Refrigerated, the paste will keep for 3–4 weeks. Although it will lose flavour over time, massaman has a longer shelf life than most pastes as it is packed-full of dry spices, as well as salt and chillies.

YELLOW CURRY PASTE

MAKES 200–300G
(3–4 SERVINGS)

GF

VE

Yellow curry originates from the southern regions of Thailand and is usually seasoned to be quite sour. This recipe is in no way traditional, as I think it benefits from first roasting some of the ingredients to give the paste a more rounded flavour.

Start by roasting the garlic, chillies and shallots. This can be done either over a barbecue or in the oven – whichever you prefer. Smoking them over wood will give the paste an intense flavoursome finish, but roasting them in the oven will still be delicious.

Preheat the oven to 180°C/gas mark 4. Roast the garlic, chillies and shallots for 25–30 minutes until softened and fragrant. Remove from the oven and set aside so they are cool enough to handle, then peel the garlic and shallots.

Using the salt as an abrasive, pount the remaining ingredients individually in a pestle and mortar. Start with the toughest ingredient, the lemongrass, and transfer each individual paste into a bowl before pounding the next ingredient. Once all are pounded individually, combine them in the mortar along with the roasted garlic, chillies and shallots to form an orangey–yellow paste.

Refrigerated, the paste will keep perfectly for 1–2 weeks in an airtight container. It will then begin to discolour, but will still be edible for another week.

Ingredients:

- 4 heads of garlic
- 20g long red chillies, stems removed and deseeded
- 100g banana shallots
- 4 sticks lemongrass, outer sheath removed, chopped into small pieces
- 1 teaspoon coarse sea salt
- 3 tablespoons peeled and sliced wild ginger
- 2 tablespoons peeled and roughly chopped fresh red turmeric (or 2 teaspoons dried turmeric)
- 2 tablespoons coriander seeds, toasted
- 1 tablespoon cumin seeds, toasted
- 2 tablespoons chopped coriander roots
- 3 tablespoons mild curry powder

RED JUNGLE CURRY PASTE

MAKES
ABOUT 800G
(4–5 SERVINGS)

GF

VE
OPTIONAL

Traditionally, jungle curry isn't cooked out with any coconut milk, since coconuts are not often found in the jungles of the Thai highlands, so it's usually very hot. It's also a very loose curry, not too dissimilar to a soup, but don't let this fool you, it packs one hell of a punch. It is often seasoned with sugar, tamarind water and fish sauce and let out with stock. I've also seen it eaten with a squeeze of fresh lime or kaffir lime juice.

Pound the fresh ingredients one at a time in a pestle and mortar until each forms a smooth paste. Start with the lemongrass and pound until it forms a paste, then repeat with the galangal, chillies, garlic, coriander root, shallots, lime leaves and gapi paste. Combine them in the mortar to form one paste, using the salt as an abrasive, which also acts as a preservative.

Store the paste in an airtight container covered with a layer of clingfilm to act as a barrier against oxidisation. If the paste turns brown, it has oxidised and the flavour will be affected. Refrigerated, the paste should keep for 2–3 weeks.

Ingredients:

- 8–10 sticks lemongrass, chopped into small pieces
- 60g galangal, peeled and roughly chopped
- 100g red bird's-eye chillies
- 100g long red chillies, stems removed and deseeded
- 150g garlic cloves, peeled
- 10g coriander roots, chopped
- 200g banana shallots, peeled and chopped into small pieces
- 8g kaffir lime leaves, stems removed and julienned
- 30g gapi (shrimp paste), roasted in oven (optional)
- 1 teaspoon coarse sea salt

163

MAKES ABOUT 1KG
(5-6 SERVINGS)

250g garlic cloves, unpeeled

250g banana shallots,
unpeeled

10g whole white peppercorns,
toasted and ground

10g coriander seeds, toasted

10g cumin seeds, toasted

60g large dried red chillies,
cut in half and soaked in
warm water to soften,
drained, deseeded as much
as possible

16 sticks lemongrass,
outer sheaths remove,
topped and tailed

100g galangal, peeled

2 tablespoons chopped
coriander roots

2 tablespoons roasted gapi
paste (fermented shrimp
paste), (optional)

a large pinch of coarse salt

ROASTED
RED CURRY PASTE

**Red curry, or *prik gaeng ped*, is incredibly popular and is
certainly one of the most commonly ordered dishes at
Farang. It provides the base to a few other curries too,
many of which feature in this book. The astonishing flavour
of a red curry paste does not just stop at a curry either.
It's found its way into stir-fries and even soups. Traditionally,
the ingredients are just finely chopped and then pounded in
a pestle and mortar. However, I like to roast the shallots and
the garlic first as it adds a worthwhile depth of flavour. If you
follow the recipe without doing this it will make a regular
red curry paste.**

**Red curry paste is normally cooked out in coconut oil and
then seasoned with fish sauce and palm sugar. This is then let
out with coconut cream and stock and served with meats,
fish or vegetables and accompanied by steamed jasmine rice.**

Roast the garlic and shallots in their skins. I like to skewer and then
grill them over a wood fire so that they take on a lovely smoky flavour.
Alternatively, you can preheat the oven to 180°C/gas mark 4 and roast
the garlic and shallots for 25–30 minutes until soft. Once softened, remove
them from the heat and allow to cool, then peel off and discard the skins.

Meanwhile, pound all the remaining ingredients, one by one, in a
large granite pestle and mortar until they each form a paste. Transfer each
individual paste into a bowl before pounding the next ingredient. Make
sure to pound the spices first while the mortar is dry to form one spice
mix and then put to one side. Alternatively, you can use a spice grinder.

Next, pound the soaked chillies as these are the toughest due to
their fibrous skins. Once you have pounded all the ingredients separately,
mix them all together, including the garlic and shallots. To speed things up
a little and if the paste doesn't all fit in the mortar, run it through a food
processor for a few minutes to ensure that all ingredients are well mixed.

Transfer to an airtight container and keep refrigerated. Because of
the salt and chilli content, this paste will keep for 3–4 weeks.

SMOKY GREEN CURRY PASTE

MAKES ABOUT 1KG
(5–6 SERVINGS)

GF

VE
OPTIONAL

Kaeng khiao wan **essentially means 'sweet green curry' (their words do not always exactly match ours meaning for meaning). Traditionally, a green curry is as hot, or a little milder, than a red curry, with a sweet and salty balance. I like to season my green curry using a little palm sugar and then let it out using stock and fresh coconut cream to create a sweet and creamy consistency.**

Now, if you have never made a curry paste from scratch before you are in for a treat. Whatever anyone says, I stand by the simple fact that a Thai curry paste, made at home, in a pestle and mortar, is a far superior product than anything you can buy. Once you get it right you will slap yourself for using flat old supermarket pastes and never use one again. Get yourself to a good oriental supermarket and you will find all the fresh, Asian produce you need to make an authentic curry paste.

In a pestle and mortar pound the fresh ingredients one at a time, using the salt as an abrasive, until each forms a smooth paste. Once all are pounded individually, combine them in the mortar to form one paste.

Toast the spices in a frying pan over a moderate heat. However, bear in mind that these all toast at different rates, so start with the coriander seeds, shaking the pan constantly. As soon as they start to s moke a little, add the mace and cumin. Toast for another minute, then add the peppercorns and remove the pan from the heat. The heat from the hot spices is enough to toast the peppercorns; if they remain on the heat they will pop and explode. Allow the spices to cool slightly, then grind them to a fine powder before adding them to the paste. Keep pestle and mortaring away until you are left with a slightly moist, fairly smooth paste, with no identifiable chunks.

Store the paste in an airtight container, covered with a layer of clingfilm to act as a barrier against oxidisation. If the paste turns brown, it has oxidised and the flavour will be affected. Refrigerated, the paste will keep for 2–3 weeks.

1–2 teaspoons coarse sea salt

8–10 sticks lemongrass, peeled, topped and tailed, outside sheath removed and sliced into small chunks

30g galangal, peeled and cut into small chunks

150g green bird's-eye chillies, stems removed, roasted over a barbecue or in the oven for about 10 minutes until softened and a little smoky

150g long green chillies, stems and seeds removed, thinly sliced, roasted over a barbecue or in the oven for about 10 minutes until softened and a little smoky

250g garlic cloves, peeled

250g Thai shallots, peeled and roughly chopped (or banana shallots)

20g coriander roots, finely sliced

30g fresh red turmeric, peeled

20g wild ginger (*krachai*), peeled and roughly chopped

1 tablespoon roasted gapi paste (fermented shrimp paste) (optional)

3 teaspoons coriander seeds

2 pieces (about 2g) mace

2 teaspoons cumin seeds

1 tablespoon whole white peppercorns

6 SWEET STUFF

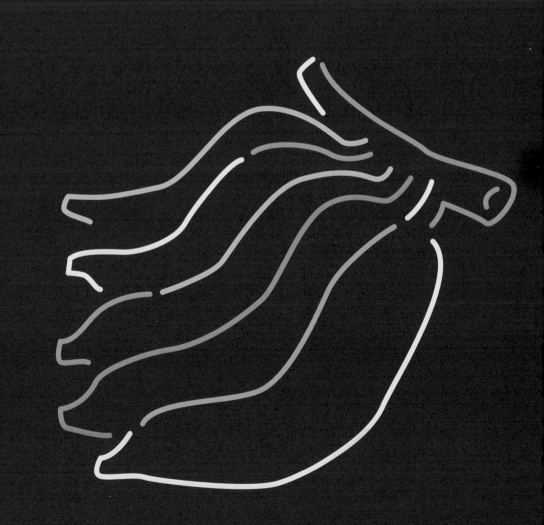

100g black (or white) glutinous rice, soaked in water for a minimum of 2 hours, ideally overnight

100g caster sugar

400g can condensed milk

5g table salt

300ml coconut cream, plus extra to serve

20g strawberries, to serve

20g raspberries, to serve

1 teaspoon sesame seeds, toasted, to garnish

BLACK RICE, SUMMER BERRIES AND COCONUT PUDDING

This is a regular at Farang, but was created by my mum, so I can't take the credit for it. And no matter how many times I try, I can't ever get it quite as good as when she makes it. I'm not sure why, but I think maybe she's hiding something. Anyway, this is the recipe that she claims to use, which comes out pretty delicious, whoever makes it.

Put the soaked rice in a large, non-stick saucepan and submerge in warm water. Place on a high heat and stir regularly to ensure the rice does not stick to the bottom of the pan. When the water level falls to lower than the rice line, top up with more hot water. Repeat this process until the rice has softened. This will take 45 minutes–1 hour; you can't overcook this rice.

When the rice has softened and the water has mostly boiled away, add the sugar, condensed milk, salt and coconut cream, and cook for a further 5 minutes until all the ingredients have infused. The rice pudding should be thick enough to stick to a spoon and taste rich, sweet and moreish. Remove from the heat and either serve immediately or cool before refrigerating. It will keep well for up to a week, but should be heated thoroughly and re-seasoned to taste with sugar and salt before eating.

Serve hot in bowls topped with the strawberries and raspberries, a drizzle of coconut cream and a sprinkling of sesame seeds.

MAKES 700ML
(6-8 SERVINGS)

180g caster sugar

a pinch of coarse sea salt

4 kaffir lime leaves, torn to
release their flavour

1 stick of lemongrass, bruised

150ml soda water

350ml lime juice (1 lime
usually yields 20–25ml)

½ small pineapple
(about 150g), peeled
and roughly diced

100ml coconut cream,
to serve

LIME GRANITA WITH FRESH PINEAPPLE, COCONUT CREAM AND SEA SALT

This works well with any fresh fruit but, if you find yourself anywhere near an Asian supermarket, stock up on rambutan, lychee and mangoes. The sharpness of the lime granita is a treat when balanced with a lovely sweet fruit.

In a large saucepan, heat 180ml water, the caster sugar, a pinch of salt, the lime leaves and lemongrass until the sugar has dissolved and the flavours have fused together; this should take 8–10 minutes on a medium heat. Discard the lime leaves and lemongrass.

Add the soda water and lime juice to the pan and stir gently (try not to stir all the bubbles out of the soda water). Pour into a freezer-proof container with a lid and freeze. Take out every hour and, using a fork, scrape the granita so that you end up with fluffy ice, rather than one big block of ice. It should take about 4 hours to freeze.

To serve, put a generous portion of pineapple in a bowl, top with a scoop of granita and pour over a little coconut cream. Sprinkle with a small pinch of sea salt.

50ml palm sugar

I tablespoon condensed milk

50ml thick tamarind water

2 bananas, sliced in half lengthways with the skins still on

I teaspoon sesame oil

¼ teaspoon flaked sea salt

GRILLED BANANAS AND TAMARIND CARAMEL

This is an awesome dessert – simple, incredibly tasty and quick to whip up. I always use a barbecue to grill my bananas, as I feel that the flavours benefit from being charred over a direct flame. However, cooking them in an oven is still delicious.

Begin by making the caramel. In a small non-stick saucepan, gently melt the palm sugar and condensed milk in the tamarind water. Continue to gently boil the mixture until the sugar begins to caramelise and the resulting caramel starts to thicken. This will not take too long, so stay with it. The caramel should be thick enough to cling to a spoon, yet loose enough to slowly pour off it.

Meanwhile, grill the bananas. Lightly coat the flesh with the sesame oil and grill for 3 minutes on each side. Grilling the skin too helps to soften the banana within. Serve the bananas with generous helpings of caramel and a sprinkling of sea salt.

SERVES 6 BIG AND
8 SMALL PEOPLE

KAFFIR LIME DOUGHNUTS
with PANDAN CUSTARD

500g plain flour,
plus extra for dusting

7g fast action dried yeast

1 teaspoon baking powder

70g unsalted butter

70g caster sugar, plus
an extra 2 tablespoons
for sprinkling

1 large egg

260ml whole milk

1 litre sunflower oil

6 kaffir lime leaves, julienned

500ml double cream

8 pandan leaves,
cut into 3cm strips

6 large egg yolks

300g caster sugar

2 teaspoons table salt

200g demerara sugar

300g sweet apples, peeled
cored and roughly chopped

These little beauties go down an absolute storm at Farang. They are also great to cook with kids as you can cut the dough into whatever shapes you like (also, for the same reason, a great recipe for big kids like myself). In Thailand, little dinosaur-shaped doughnuts are common, though mine never seem to get more intricate than basic circles. Oh well, it's the taste that counts, right?

Sift the flour, yeast and baking powder into a bowl and rub in the butter, then add the sugar. In a separate bowl, beat the egg and milk together. Make a well in the flour mixture, pour in the egg and milk, and mix to form a soft dough. Allow to prove for 1 hour in a warm, dry place. Roll out the dough on a well-floured surface to about 1cm thick and cut into shapes of your choice. The dough will make 15–20 golf ball-sized doughnuts.

Meanwhile, heat the oil to 180°C in a deep, wide saucepan. To check the oil is the right temperature, drop in a small piece of dough; if the dough gently bubbles and floats to the top, then the oil is ready. Fry 5–6 doughnuts at a time for about 2 minutes, then flip them over and fry for a further 1½ minutes until golden brown all over. Carefully remove them from the oil using a slotted spoon and drain on kitchen paper, then sprinkle with the caster sugar and kaffir lime leaves while still hot.

Next, gently heat the cream and the pandan leaves in a saucepan. When hot, whizz in a food processor or blender to break up the pandan leaves so that they release their colour and flavour into the cream, then strain back into the pan. Beat the egg yolks into the caster sugar until the mixture turns pale yellow and thick. Then, very slowly, add this to the warm cream while whisking constantly. The slower you add the egg/sugar mixture, the less likely it will split, so go very carefully. Once combined, return the pan to a low heat and cook, stirring, until the mixture turns light green and thickens, but still stays pourable. Stir in 1 teaspoon of the salt.

Lastly, place the demerara sugar, apples and the remaining teaspoon of salt in a saucepan with about 50ml cold water and simmer until the apples are soft and the sugar is caramelised.

Serve the freshly cooked doughnuts with the custard and the apple jam on top and get stuck in. If you want to show off you can use a jam injector but in my opinion there is no need.

PANDAN SPONGE CAKE

200g caster sugar

50g pandan leaves, chopped into small pieces

½ teaspoon salt

70g corn oil

100g plain flour

50ml coconut milk

6 medium eggs, separated

The first time I tried this was after a visit to London's Chinatown. I often find myself excitedly exploring the shops for new things to try and was attracted to pandan cake due to its bright green colour. After taking it home and eating the entire thing in one sitting, I realised that it was something I need more of in my life, so I learnt how to make it.

Start by making the pandan juice. In a medium saucepan, heat 200ml water with 100g of the sugar, the pandan leaves and salt and simmer gently. Remove from the heat and use a hand-held blender or food processor to break up the pandan leaves into the sugary water to release their flavour and colour. Return the pan to the heat and continue to simmer to fully infuse the flavour. When the water has reduced by half, strain the leaves from the syrup. This should leave you with 100ml pandan juice.

Line the base of a 20cm round cake tin with parchment paper but do not grease the sides. Heat the oil in a large saucepan to a simmer; it should reach about 70°C. Remove from the heat, immediately add the flour and stir with a whisk until smooth. Add the coconut milk and pandan juice and stir to combine. At this stage the batter will become thick and lumpy.

Add the egg yolks and whisk with a hand whisk until the batter is smooth and runny again. Set aside. In a bowl, beat the egg whites until foamy, then gradually whisk in the remaining sugar until soft peaks forms and the mixture is thick enough to stick to a spoon but still smooth enough to run off it.

Add one-third of the whites into the yolk batter and use a hand whisk to ensure the mixtures are thoroughly combined. Add the next third portion and continue whisking. Finally, add the last third and whisk briefly before switching to a spatula to scrape the batter from the bottom of the pan to make sure everything is combined and no yolk batter can be seen.

Preheat the oven to 190°C/gas mark 5. Pour the mixture into the prepared cake tin and then place the tin in a water bath, making sure that the water only comes half way up the sides of the tin so the water does not bubble over into the batter. Bake in the water bath at 190°C for 15 minutes before lowering the temperature to 145°C/gas mark 1 for another hour, or until the top of the cake bounces back when lightly pressed. Remove from the oven and leave to cool for 20 minutes before turning out. The cake will keep for a week, kept in the fridge.

SWEET STUFF

CONDENSED MILK AND GREEN TEA ICE CREAM

MAKES ABOUT 750G
(5-6 SERVINGS)

VE

7 egg yolks

50g palm sugar

½ teaspoon table salt

250g condensed milk

6 pandan leaves, roughly chopped

20g dried green tea leaves, pounded to a fine powder

500ml double cream

This ice cream is absolutely banging and very easy to make without using an ice cream maker. For me, anything with condensed milk in it is already a winner, and the fresh burst of green tea really complements the richness. I like to use pandan leaves, too, as it changes the colour and flavour of the ice cream. However, it can be left out and is still delicious.

Begin by whisking together the egg yolks, palm sugar and salt in a large metal bowl until thick and full of air. The eggs will turn a slightly pale colour because of the air content, which is a tell-tale sign that they are ready.

Meanwhile, heat the condensed milk in a heatproof bowl set over a pan of gently simmering water, stirring regularly to ensure that the milk does not stick to the bowl. Add the pandan leaves and, when warm, blitz in a food processor so that their flavour is released into the condensed milk, which will turn green. Strain the mixture and discard any large pieces of pandan.

Very gradually, add the milk to the egg yolks, whisking constantly to gently warm the eggs. Don't add too much warm milk at a time, otherwise the eggs will scramble. Transfer this mixture back into the heatproof bowl and return to the heat over the simmering water, stirring constantly to stop the eggs from scrambling or sticking to the bowl. Heat for 4–5 minutes until the mixture is the consistency of custard; there should be no lumps. Now stir in the green tea leaves. Place a piece of parchment paper on the surface of the mixture to stop a skin from forming, then cool for 15–20 minutes before transferring to the fridge.

Using an electric hand whisk, whisk the double cream until it forms soft peaks. The cream should be thick enough to cling to a spoon, yet loose enough to slowly slide off it. Gently fold the double cream into the condensed milk mixture, making sure not to knock out all the air.

Transfer the mixture to a freezer-proof container and place in the freezer. Take the mixture out every 2 hours and give it a gentle whisk. This distributes the ice crystals as the mixture freezes, making a smoother, easier-to-scoop ice cream. The ice cream will take 6–8 hours to fully freeze, depending on the freezer.

MANGO JAM CAKE

210g plain flour

1 teaspoon baking powder

½ teaspoon baking soda

½ teaspoon allspice

¼ teaspoon ground cardamom

¼ teaspoon ground cloves

¼ teaspoon table salt

170g brown sugar

6 tablespoons unsalted butter, plus extra for greasing

2 medium eggs

30g soured cream

FOR THE MANGO JAM

5 medium mangoes, plus extra slices to garnish

2 lemons, peeled (keep the peel and flesh)

300g brown sugar

a pinch of salt

This is another of my creations, and always goes down a storm. It's the result of having had way too many mangoes in the kitchen; I'm not sure who ordered them. So, as I hate waste, I made a jam that tasted bloody lovely. From that, the jam was used in a cake, which is now one of my favourite dessert recipes. It's awesome with ice cream. Overripe mangoes are perfect.

Start by making the mango jam. Peel the mangoes and put them whole in a large saucepan. Add the lemon peel and flesh to the pan, cover the fruits with the sugar and a pinch of salt and then cook over a medium heat, stirring regularly. Keep stirring on a medium–low heat for about 30 minutes, or until you see the rolling boil happening and the mango flesh has detached itself from the stones and only the strings are left. Be sure to keep an eye on the jam as it has a tendency to stick to the base of the pan.

Test the jam by dropping a small blob of it onto a cold plate. If the jam is too runny, it will need more cooking time; if it clings to the plate and a thin skin forms, it is ready. Discard the lemon peel, lemons, mango stones and strings.

Preheat the oven to 180°C/gas mark 4. Sift the flour, baking powder and baking soda into a large bowl. Add the allspice, ground cardamom, ground cloves and salt, then mix well and set aside.

Using an electric mixer (or hand-held electric whisk), cream the brown sugar and butter together until smooth. Add the eggs, one at a time, and the soured cream. Using a rubber spatula, fold the flour mix and spices into the cream mixture then stir in two-thirds of the mango jam and mix until all the ingredients are well combined. Pour the batter into a lightly greased 22cm springform cake tin and gently tap the tin on the counter a few times to release any trapped air.

Bake the cake in the oven for 25–30 minutes. Test for doneness by inserting a sharp knife or skewer into the centre of the cake – if it comes out clean the cake is cooked all the way through. Turn the cake out onto a wire rack and leave to cool completely, then spread a thin layer of the remaining mango jam over the top and garnish with fresh mango slices. Serve straight away, or keep refrigerated and eat within 2–3 days.

3 tablespoons palm sugar, broken into small pieces

I teaspoon table salt

2 pandan leaves, tied in a knot

250g cashew nuts

PALM SUGAR GLAZED SALTED CASHEW NUTS

This recipe is a cross between a bar snack and a dessert. You can use fish sauce instead of water and sprinkle the cashews with dried shrimp floss instead of salt to make it a more savoury nibble. Or try with peanuts and pistachios.

In a small bowl, combine the palm sugar, half the salt and the pandan leaves with 2 tablespoons cold water. Stir to combine, but don't worry that the sugar and salt won't all be dissolved at this stage. Set this next to your cooker so you are ready to go, as you will need to move fast!

In a medium–large saucepan, toast the cashews over a medium heat for 6–8 minutes, stirring regularly to prevent them burning and to ensure even toasting. When you start smelling a lovely nutty aroma, quickly drizzle the sugar mixture over the cashews, stirring the nuts as you pour. Move the nuts around the pan constantly for about 15 seconds, until the cashews are thoroughly coated in the sugar mixture, then immediately remove the pan from heat so that they don't burn.

Spread the cashews out on a piece of parchment paper, carefully remove the pandan leaves and leave to cool. Sprinkle very lightly with the rest of the table salt. You can break the nuts apart, if you like.

Enjoy immediately or store in an airtight container. The cashews will be slightly sticky at first, but the coating hardens within a few hours.

MALTOSE, WHITE CHOCOLATE AND COCONUT MOUSSE

50ml coconut cream

25g maltose

200ml double cream

100g white chocolate

2 egg whites

20g desiccated coconut, toasted, to serve

This is my own little creation, and is the perfect dessert when you're in a rush, as it doesn't take long. Using coconut cream alongside maltose works in perfect harmony, so give it a try.

Place a large metal bowl over a saucepan of simmering water. Add the coconut cream, maltose, double cream and chocolate to the bowl and heat gently, stirring regularly until the chocolate has melted into a smooth mixture with no lumps. Remove from the heat, place a circle of parchment paper directly onto the surface of the mixture to avoid it forming a skin, and refrigerate.

In a large bowl, whisk the egg whites until stiff and holding their shape, then gently fold through the cold creamy chocolate mixture, making sure not to knock any air out of the mousse.

Pour the mixture into ramekins or serving bowls and leave to set in the fridge for 2 hours. Sprinkle with the coconut just before serving.

SWEET STUFF

BANANA AND
CONDENSED MILK ROTIS

SERVES 4 VE

270g plain flour, sifted

a pinch of coarse sea salt, crushed to fine powder

I large egg, beaten

200ml warm water

olive oil, for greasing

4 bananas, peeled and sliced in half lengthways and widthways

3 tablespoons caster sugar

2 tablespoons soft unsalted butter

100g condensed milk, to serve

You can now find an endless array of delicious fillings and coatings for roti, both sweet and savoury. What began as just a simple condensed milk and sugar filling, has now evolved to include bananas, strawberry jam and Nutella. Apparently you can even get pizza toppings (not that I have seen this with my own eyes). These days, pretty much anything goes, but in my opinion you can't beat the good old classic banana roti.

Start by making the roti dough. Add the sifted flour, salt and egg to a mixing bowl, then rub together using your fingers until the mixture is the consistency of breadcrumbs. Little by little, add the water to the bowl and knead for 8–10 minutes. The dough should be tacky but not sticking to the bowl or your fingers. This dough is quite wet compared to regular bread dough.

Lightly oil a bowl and place the dough in it; this ensures the dough does not stick to the bowl during the resting process. Cover the dough with clingfilm, making sure the clingfilm is in direct contact with the dough to stop it crusting over. Leave to rest for a minimum of 30 minutes.

Meanwhile, preheat the oven to 180°C/gas mark 4. Line a tray with parchment paper and place the bananas on the tray. Sprinkle with 2 tablespoons of the sugar, then transfer to the oven for 8–10 minutes. The bananas are ready when the sugar has turned golden brown and the bananas are soft.

Now for the fun bit: cooking the rotis. If you're feeling ambitious, then try the traditional method of slapping out the roti dough. Lightly oil a clean surface. Shape the dough mix with your hands into balls, roughly double the size of a golf ball. You'll have enough spare dough to have a few attempts so don't worry too much about not getting it right first time.

Place the ball of dough on the oiled surface. Flatten it into a rough circular shape, then gently lift the side closest to you and pull it towards you. Lift quickly but delicately and slap the dough back onto the surface (its elasticity and stickiness mean that it won't tear too easily and stretches as you pull it). Repeat this process until the dough is 2–3mm thick (the thinner the better, but don't make it too hard to lift into the pan, a few holes are fine). Alternatively, use a rolling pin. I have watched many chefs attempt this process and none, including myself, got it perfect first time, so don't worry if it all goes a little pear-shaped, it will still taste amazing.

Meanwhile, heat half the butter in a large frying pan to a medium heat (the butter needs to be really hot in order to crisp the dough, but don't burn it). Carefully place the dough into the pan; if it sizzles you're doing it right. As soon as the dough starts to cook, place a softened banana in the centre. Fold the sides of the dough over into a rectangle shape and then flip over, adding a little more butter if needed. Fry for about 3 minutes on each side until the roti is golden brown and crispy on both sides. Repeat this process with the remaining rotis. Serve immediately topped with the condensed milk and remaining sugar.

STICKY MANGO WITH PALM SUGAR CARAMEL

200g glutinous rice

400ml coconut cream

150g caster sugar

150g palm sugar

50ml condensed milk

5g toasted black sesame seeds

a pinch of table salt

2 ripe mangoes (soft to the touch but not bruised)

Sticky mango pudding is the type of thing that you put in your mouth and think, 'Where the fuck has this been all my life?' More please! It has a naughty, rich sweetness to it from the coconut cream and condensed milk, topped with a seemingly healthy slice of fresh mango and palm sugar caramel. In fact, it couldn't be more moreish. I've made a few adaptations to the standard version, as I think the flavours of a bitter salted palm sugar caramel over the top takes the dish to the next level.

Put the rice in a sieve and run it under cold water for 1 minute, then submerge the rinsed rice in warm water for 20 minutes. Meanwhile, set up a rice steamer. (If you don't have one, a saucepan half-filled with water with a colander placed over it works well. When the water is hot, put clingfilm over the colander to create a steamer.)

When the water is boiling, reduce the heat to medium and add the soaked sticky rice to the steamer or colander (check that the rice is not blocking all the holes in the steamer before you put the lid on, otherwise the steam won't surround the rice and it will not cook). The rice should take 20–25 minutes to cook. Check that the grains are soft throughout before removing the rice from the heat.

Meanwhile, in a saucepan, heat the coconut cream and caster sugar over a medium heat to melt the sugar and loosen the coconut cream. When warm, add the cooked sticky rice and combine using a whisk, then put clingfilm over the pan; the heat from the hot rice will help the rice absorb the sweet coconut liquid. Leave covered for at least 10 minutes to ensure the rice swells to a nice thick consistency.

Add the palm sugar and condensed milk to a small saucepan and bring to the boil over a high heat, stirring constantly for 3–4 minutes to allow the sugar to caramelise and thicken. The mixture is ready when it takes on a honey-like consistency and pours off a spoon slowly. At the same time, warm the sesame seeds in a 180°C/gas mark 4 oven for about 2 minutes, then sprinkle with the salt.

Peel the mangoes, then slice as close as possible along either side of the flat stone so that you end up with a total of 4 mango halves. Then slice the halves into bite-sized pieces.

To serve, divide the rice between 4 plates and top with the mangoes. Pour over the palm sugar caramel, sprinkle with the toasted sesame seeds and serve immediately.

INDEX

ACKNOWLEDGEMENTS

Firstly, I would like to thank my awesome mum, who has always been the engine room of my business and fuelled my passion for food; from running restaurants to washing kitchen towels, she's always doing something to make my life easier.

I would also like to thank my girlfriend, Sinead, who always manages to deal with my shit; even when I decide to write a book and open a restaurant at the same time, and then find myself too busy to remember to put shoes on before leaving the house, she somehow finds a way to pick up the pieces.

Thanks to the entire team at Kyle Books for doing such a cracking job, most importantly Kyle and Judith for getting as excited about *Cook Thai* as I was from the beginning and giving me everything I needed to make the cookbook I had envisioned a reality. Thanks also to Tom Regester, as his photography throughout this book is flawless; Becks Wilkinson for her rock star attitude and complete professionalism and Luis Peral. I don't think writing a cookbook can get much better than writing it with this team – they smashed it!

Thank you to my amazing agents Borra Garson and Louise Leftwich at DML who have helped guide me in the right direction over the last few years. This book and many other things would not be possible if it wasn't for their constant hard work and dedication.

A huge thank you to all the people who contributed to this book: Andy Oliver, Henry Dimbleby, Nigel Barden, Annitta Potter, Deirdre Kane, Dan Turner, Narisa Chauvidul-Aw and the Thai Embassy. Also to those who didn't have the time but who I would have loved to be in it: Craig Broadhurst, Luke Farrell, Jane Alty. You are all the reasons I love cooking Thai food and I am honoured to have you (or to have nearly had you, ha) in my book.

Some huge thanks are in order for my whole Farang team, who always work their arses off to make our food something special, most importantly Dan, Ross and Josh who kept the ship afloat whilst I was scratching my head in front of a computer writing this book over the last year, also I can't forget Phil who cooked with me and Dan at the very beginning before moving to Mexico and played a large part in Farang being what it is today.

I would also like to thank my stepfather, Marko Fossaluzza, for always offering his words of wisdom when I hit a hurdle in the business, and for letting me use his house as a production kitchen before I could afford my own (even though I'm not sure he ever really gave me consent?).

I would also like to thank my grandad, dad and Polly for giving me the financial help I needed to start up my own business from pretty much nothing.

Also a special thanks to Frank, Kare and Nikki Groves for your constant support over the years and Sean Groves for your ability to build barbecues overnight in car parks for Farang.

And last, but not least, I would like to thank my friends back home in Oxford and my family across the country for their constant support, especially my brother and sister who will always be there to lovingly eat my food without paying for any of it, and Max who always comes to all my events despite being a vegan and only being able to eat a few dishes (I have made sure you have lots to cook in this book). Without all of you guys I would have no reason to have written this book at all and I hope to see it get dusty on your book shelves forever after.